YORK MEDIEVAL TEXTS

General Editors

ELIZABETH SALTER & DEREK PEARSALL

University of York

P9-DFH-483

For Sarah

᚛᚛᚛᚛᚛᚛᚛᚛᚛᚛᚛᚛᚛᚛᚛

The Morte Darthur

᚛᚛᚛᚛᚛᚛᚛᚛᚛᚛᚛᚛᚛᚛᚛

PARTS SEVEN AND EIGHT

by

Sir THOMAS MALORY

Edited with an Introduction,
Notes and Glossary by

D. S. BREWER

University Lecturer in English
Fellow of Emmanuel College, Cambridge

Northwestern University Press
Evanston

Northwestern University Press
Evanston, Illinois 60208–4210

Copyright © D. S. Brewer 1968. First published in Great Britain by Edward
Arnold (Publishers) Ltd. First published in the United States of America in 1968
by Northwestern University Press. All rights reserved.

Second paperback printing 1975
Third paperback printing 1977
Fourth paperback printing 1978
Fifth paperback printing 1981
Sixth paperback printing 1983
Seventh paperback printing 1985
Eighth paperback printing 1989
Ninth paperback printing 1995
Tenth paperback printing 1996

Library of Congress Catalog Card Number 68:22420
ISBN 0–8101–0031–2

Preface

The present series of *York Medieval Texts* is designed for undergraduates and, where the text is appropriate, for upper forms of schools. Its aim is to provide editions of major pieces of Middle English writing in a form which will make them accessible without loss of historical authenticity. Texts are chosen because of their importance and artistic merit, and individual volumes may contain a single work, coherent extracts from a longer work, or representative examples of a genre. The principle governing the presentation of the text is to preserve the character of the English while eliminating unnecessary encumbrances such as obsolete letters and manuscript errors. Glossary and explanatory notes operate together to clarify the text; special attention is paid to the interpretation of passages which are syntactically rather than lexically difficult. The Introduction to each volume, like the rest of the apparatus, is designed to set the work in its proper literary context, and to provide the critical guidance most helpful to present-day readers. The intention of the series is exclusively literary: the Editors hope to attract a wider audience not only for works within the accepted literary canon, but also for those which have until now been regarded as 'specialist' in appeal, or which have been presented as if they were.

There is little need specially to commend *The Morte Darthur*. It has been known for centuries as a superb story of adventure and love, honour and betrayal, able to keep children from play and old men from the chimney-corner. Only literary critics have neglected it. It is a long and complex work, during the writing of which Malory perfected his art, and the earlier parts, excellent as they are, have not quite the dramatic power and the pervasive deep tragic irony of the story of passion, war and society that constitutes the last quarter of the book; and perhaps critics have not appreciated the difference. By presenting this last quarter, which has its own natural unity within the larger whole, the present edition focuses more sharply on the greatness of Malory's achievement, and allows the reader to see it and enjoy it more readily. With a similar aim the spelling is modernized, because the vagaries of late fifteenth-century spelling are merely distracting to the modern reader. But the actual words and basic forms are preserved, and the student need have no fear that modernization has been carried so far as to obscure the finer nuances of Malory's style. The text is based on the Winchester Manuscript, corrected by reference to Caxton's text, and is, in intention, as close to Malory's original as we can get.

The Introduction summarizes what the reader needs to know about the Arthurian story and Arthurian scholarship in order to understand and enjoy Malory's work, but the main emphasis is on Malory's own writing, which still deserves more literary study. The sections on Style, Structure, and the Tragedy of the Honourable Society are original contributions to the criticism of *The Morte Darthur*.

Acknowledgements

My debt to previous scholars is suggested in the footnotes and Bibliography, but no one can work on Malory now without being intensely aware of a special debt to Professor Vinaver's edition of the *Works*, to whose riches I have had constant recourse. The text of this modernized edition is based upon that of Professor Vinaver's *Works of Sir Thomas Malory* (Oxford Standard Authors, 1954), with some checking against a microfilm of the Winchester Manuscript and with Caxton's text. I should also like to express my thanks to the General Editors for valuable suggestions and guidance, and to Miss R. McQuillan whose secretarial help has eased many burdens. I am also much indebted to the Warden and Fellows of Winchester College for allowing me to study the Winchester Manuscript through the medium of a microfilm.

Contents

Introduction

Malory's series of stories has delighted five centuries of readers, whether or not their own lives have been as exciting as his book. The Arthurian tales, that mixture of myth, adventure, love-story, enchantment, tragedy, live in his work as the essence of medieval romance, yet always with a contemporary relevance. This combination of romantic remoteness with contemporary relevance was true even in his own day. He wrote in the middle of the fifteenth century, a period of sagging confidence, and bewildering change, when England's empire had been almost entirely lost. He was looking backward to an imagined, more primitive, if glorious past. Contemplation of this past, however, was to provide, besides its intrinsic interest, an analysis of the problems of the present, and also an ideal for the future.[1] *The Morte Darthur* was a part of the movement that transformed the medieval knight into the English gentleman. It expresses those potent ideals of the gentleman's private virtue and public service that despite many failings activated English society and influence up to the first half of the twentieth century.

Even in the present day we respond to Malory's art and intent. The circumstances of knights in armour are remote from us, and interesting in their remoteness, yet the symbolic power of *The Morte Darthur* can also speak to the enduring contemporary need to reconcile the individual's demands with those of society, to recognize and cherish personal integrity, and true love, and to create a good society. Nothing bears witness more strikingly to the human power of Malory's work than the way it haunts the imagination of modern writers. Hardly a year passes without some retelling of the tale.

The Arthurian legend, in remotest origins Celtic, a medieval best-seller in twelfth-century Latin, which developed in the various European vernaculars into perhaps the largest single body of imaginative literature that the world has known, survives into the modern world as a living work only in English, at the hands of almost its last remodeller, Sir Thomas Malory. It is one of the many paradoxes of *The Morte Darthur* that it both is and is not Malory's. He is very much a translator, and rarely moves without help from sources. Yet he is also fully independent in handling his sources and unquestionably a great artist. He has suffered somewhat at the hands of critics by often being read in the light of other writers with different aims. We must recognize that his book

---

[1] See Ferguson. Bibliographical references are normally denoted by key-names which are set out in alphabetical order with full references in the bibliography below, p. 41.

is built up on the foundations of earlier works, or we shall misunderstand its nature, but it is the aim of the present essay to consider *The Morte Darthur* in its own right, as a great work of art. Many generations of readers, including men of genius and affairs from Henry VIII to T. E. Lawrence, have valued it, but literary critics from Ascham onwards have usually deplored or ignored it, misunderstanding its nature or assuming it to be merely derivative. Its real power and grasp as a book in itself have yet to be fully evaluated. Although it is the aim of this introductory essay to further that evaluation, and some new judgments are made, its brevity necessarily leaves many things only suggested or partly developed.

Malory's blend of fantasy and relevance is reinforced by his formal directness, whereby he reduces the complex elaborations of earlier Arthurian storytellers to a sequence of coherent tales which draws the reader along. Caxton, his first editor and publisher (whose edition of 1485 was for almost five centuries the only source of Malory's text), confused this strong direct form by dividing it, as he tells us, into twenty-one books, and into many, often illogical, chapter-divisions. Only when an unedited manuscript was discovered in Winchester College Library in 1934[2] was it possible to see without distraction Malory's true form, whereby the whole book is divided into eight main parts with subsections. No doubt the essential clarity of Malory's design has always been grasped, if unconsciously, by the common sense of readers, in Johnson's phrase, 'uncorrupted by literary prejudice', since Malory's book is the only version of the huge corpus of medieval Arthurian literature that is still naturally current. The other versions, more sophisticated in art and learning, have become immured within their own mazes, to which specialists alone have the key. Nevertheless, our natural appreciation of Malory's work has very much benefited now that the Winchester Manuscript is available, presented with all Professor Vinaver's learning in his splendid edition, though Professor Vinaver in his reaction from Caxton, seems in his turn to have gone beyond Malory's intentions by creating absolute divisions between the eight sections, putting asunder what Malory had carefully joined together. The text offered in this edition presents an integral portion of Malory's great work, that is, the last two main parts, where the whole work, and Malory's own art, rise to their climax. The text is taken principally from the Winchester Manuscript, occasionally corrected by reference to Caxton, except for the final pages of the manuscript, which are missing, and which therefore have to be taken from Caxton alone. The text is modernized in spelling. Little is lost by this and much is gained. Most modern English spellings would be recognizable, and many were current, in the fifteenth century, but the vagaries of fifteenth century

[2] By Mr. W. F. Oakeshott. See his account in Bennett.

spelling are distracting for the modern reader, interposing a veil of irrelevant quaintness.

II

The Growth of Arthurian Legend

The true nature of Malory's book can hardly be appreciated without recognizing how different its situation is, and was, from a modern book, particularly a novel. Most people nowadays know a bit about the Arthurian legend before they read Malory, and this has always been the case. If we pick up a modern novel, on the other hand, we are disgusted if we find that we know the story, and that parts are even copied from earlier novels. Modern novelists, poets, dramatists, must, in the significant words of Ezra Pound, 'make it new'. Before the eighteenth century writing was different. Shakespeare, for example, always used earlier writings as a base, sometimes hardly changing a word, as in his description of Cleopatra, taken from North's Plutarch. None of the great earlier writers, English or European, sought new material as the modern novelist must, or must pretend to. The same stories were constantly rewritten. For example, the story of King Lear had been told, though often very briefly, more than fifty times before Shakespeare wrote his play, which itself may have been founded on a previous play on the same subject. In this respect imaginative writers were more like modern historians than modern novelists. They sought novelty and freshness, of course, but they sought it in presentation, in taking a different view of known facts, in presenting new evidence. The similarity with historians must not be pressed too far. Older writers invented their new evidence as modern historians do not. But it may be recalled that those who are still accounted the greatest historians, Thucydides and Tacitus, certainly invented the speeches they put into the mouths of historical characters, just as Malory invented some of the speeches he put into the mouth of his main 'historical' character, King Arthur.

Such an attitude to writing as Malory's has important results. First, every reader can be expected to know the story roughly, at least. The author need not worry too much about 'unity' (see below, p. 22). He has received a given mass of material. Again, he need waste no time in building up certain effects, because they are already known, as the characters, in outline, are known, too, and he can rely on the reader's co-operation. He can achieve effects of irony and distance, along with familiarity. The author is also limited. He may change the quality of personality of a given character in the story (some writers even degraded the character of King Arthur), or the interpretation of an event, but he can hardly change a principal event completely. Secondly, the writer, taking

over a story perhaps already elaborated several times, is taking over a structure
of several layers. The advantage of this is that several layers may have effects
both powerful and obscure, surviving underneath more superficial and recent
though equally interesting layers of event and commentary, much as an oil
painting by a great master has a play of different tones through the several
layers of paint (the painted-out first thoughts and mistakes, even the dirt and
varnishes of later years may contribute to the final effect). On the other hand,
the disadvantage of an old and much rewritten story is that it may incorporate
misunderstood earlier passages; or passages from earlier and later rewritings
may be inconsistent with each other. The classic examples of such incon-
sistencies are to be found in Shakespeare's *Hamlet*. The example of *Hamlet* also
suggests that such inconsistencies are not very important in a work of art. They
violate that realism or naturalism that the nineteenth-century has taught us to
demand, but which the twentieth century, in art as in literature, is teaching us
to abandon. We must abandon it also for Malory. *The Morte Darthur*, whatever
it is, is not a novel, with the typical novel's unity and naturalism. It is a complex,
layered structure of great fascination, with its own internal laws (see further,
p. 20 below).

How do these layers come about?[3] The origin seems to have been a successful
Romanized British (i.e., in modern terms, Welsh) war-leader of the British,
or Gaelic, peoples, whom the Anglo-Saxons were conquering or driving out
of what is now England, in the fifth century A.D. The first account of Arthur
is in the story of the wars between the British and the English given by Nennius,
a British (i.e. Welsh) priest, who wrote his *Historiae Britonum* about 800.
Another mention of Arthur, however, comes in a Welsh poem perhaps of the
seventh century. Other later historians preserve and slightly extend Nennius's
account and Mordred appears as Arthur's last enemy. Other Welsh poems
show Arthur as a mythical hero, in a supernatural world, capable of strange
exploits, but already accompanied by Kay and Bedivere.

History and legend in various forms are the two chief elements in the
Arthurian story, with now one dominating, now the other, now each in
balance. History and legend were brought together for the first time in the same
work by Geoffrey of Monmouth (his origin is significant) in his *History of the
Kings of Britain* written in Latin and usually dated near 1135. It may be said of
Geoffrey's combination of the two elements that it was achieved by giving
legend the sober presentation of history. It is a fascinating situation. Geoffrey,
whose parents may have been Bretons, was probably born in Monmouth and
educated at Oxford; he wrote in Latin for a Norman-French audience, about a

---

[3] The many problems are the subject of a vast scholarly literature, most of
which has little relevance to Malory. The most useful brief and interesting
account is in Loomis (1). For fuller details see Loomis (2) and its bibliographies.

Welsh hero, who was king of England. Geoffrey derived Arthur's ancestry from a line of kings which included Lear and Cymbeline, went back to the grandson of Aeneas, called Brutus, and so back again to Romans and Trojans. His work was immensely successful in England and Europe.

The tangled skein of European culture was further interwoven by the enthusiasm with which European courts took up Geoffrey's account of Arthur. More Celtic legends were garnered from the Welsh, or from Brittany, to enrich the harvest. The Arthurian concept was so strong that it attracted other stories, of remote and separate origin, like that of Tristram. Elements from classical Latin literature, and a certain sophistication of literary culture, were employed in making Arthurian tales by clerkly court poets, especially by the French poet Chrestien of Troyes. Chrestien was probably the most influential writer—the invention of Lancelot and his love for Guenevere are perhaps his— but all the major European vernaculars produced many Arthurian stories. Although the stories are so numerous and varied, the significant point they have in common is that they used Arthurian mythology to provide a mirror in which to see the romance of their own lives, the lives of knights and ladies. Orthodox Christian story could not be so completely adopted partly because of its intrinsic nature, partly for historical reasons (though one must not forget the importance of saints' lives in the development of romance). Every society has an imaginative need to see itself, not quite as it is, but as it essentially thinks of itself. Medieval courtly European society imagined its secular self in terms of knight-errantry, conflict, love of ladies, high ideals of noble behaviour. The developing individualism of the twelfth century relished the presentation of a single knight's solitary quest, of his personal initiative, freedom from social pressures; it required the record of victories not only over normal enemies and competitors but also over monsters that are really the indwelling terrors of men's own minds. That the day-to-day actuality was often different from the literature need hardly surprise us—the same is true of novels in relation to ordinary life even today. We read novels because we hope both to lose and to find ourselves. Literature, fortunately, is not life. The fantasies of chivalric romance, especially those of Chrestien, clearly met important imaginative needs in their own time, and are attractive even now. In them, however, the element of legend, which from the twelfth century we had better call romance, predominated. The realism is limited, the historical and social elements subordinate.

From the point of view of Malory's work it is the French and a few later English versions that are important. In the thirteenth century the verse romances of Chrestien and others were turned into French prose and much enlarged, for example, by the story of Lancelot's early years, by accounts of Merlin, and by much else besides. The most important additions are the books of the

History of the Holy Grail and the *Quest of the Holy Grail*. The Grail was thought to be the vessel in which Christ's blood from the cross was received, though scholars have sought the history of the idea in pagan Gaelic culture. The intention of the Grail stories is to denigrate the chivalric life of the knight-errant and to exalt its complete opposite, the virginal, ascetic, meditative, untravelled life of the monk. The authors are thought to have been Cistercian monks. They used the chivalric myths to deny chivalric values. They wrote a serious allegorical parody of wordly chivalry to exemplify the unwordly life of the spirit. Nothing more clearly shows the tremendous imaginative power of the myth of chivalry. The Grail stories were apparently as successful as the other Arthurian stories in French prose in the thirteenth century, partly because of their literary art, and, partly, no doubt, because their audience, unlike their authors, were able to believe in *both* the chivalric virtues *and* in spiritual virtues. Most people live with such inconsistencies easily enough and no one avoids them. The Grail stories were joined with other principal Arthurian stories, such as those of Lancelot and Guenevere (a romance of adultery), and of the death of Arthur. Thus a huge composite series of romances was put together, now known, because of its popularity, as the Vulgate. The Vulgate romances are also sometimes known as 'cyclic' romances, because of the way they were narrated, by a method also known as interlacing. That is, the story of one knight was told for a few pages. Then he was left, and the tale of another taken up for a similar space. Then again a third, and so back to the first. It was these cyclic romances of the French Vulgate version that Malory knew, and that provided him with most of his material.

They may not have given him his original inspiration. They are deficient in practical historical realism and directness. These qualities Malory found nearer home, particularly in *Morte Arthure*, an alliterative poem written in English in the fourteenth century. From the middle of the fourteenth century till sometime in the fifteenth century a number of English poems are found in the alliterative metre that goes back to Old English times. At first they seem to be associated more with the Northern and Western parts of the country. They usually have a strong, provincial, old-fashioned, patriotic, aristocratic seriousness with considerable political and religious interests. Such at least is the case with the alliterative *Morte Arthure*.[4] Several of the alliterative poems show a patriotic interest in Arthur, but the alliterative *Morte* treats his triumph and death

[4] There are some variations from this pattern, naturally, in the greatest of these poems, *Piers Plowman*, which is clerical and London-based, and not aristocratic, and in the varied works of the *Gawain*-poet. In the fifteenth and sixteenth centuries alliterative verse spread widely, and was reabsorbed into the national tradition. Cf. D. S. Brewer, 'An Unpublished Late Alliterative Poem', *English Philological Studies* (1965).

extensively. In this poem the author goes back to the original historical concept of Arthur, though he knows something of later romance. Gawain, not Lancelot, is Arthur's principal knight, and there is no love-interest. Lancelot is a minor figure. What is most striking is that although Arthur is king of 'Britain', he is thought and spoken of as English, as 'our' king, his men 'our' men. It is a poem of characteristically English self-glorification—Arthur creates an Empire from Ireland to Rome—and equally characteristic self-castigation, for Arthur is criticized as well as glorified. The English audience is expected to identify itself with Arthur and his men, and it is possible that Arthur himself is quite deliberately designed to represent in certain ways Edward III (who was himself a keen Arthurian).[5] In other words, we have in this poem that sense of historical and political relevance on English ground that the French romances so notably lack. Such fantasy as there is in the alliterative *Morte*, like Arthur's fight with the giant, is presented with military realism, not untouched by a grim humour. Other elements of fantasy are presented through dream, the most realistic method of presenting fantasy. One of Arthur's dreams is of Fortune's Wheel, central to the tragic concept of the poem, as it is to the form that Malory eventually adopted.

Malory translated *Morte Arthure*. He made a number of changes in it. For example, he suppressed much of the heroic Gawain, and in turn exalted Lancelot, inventing new episodes to his glory. Since Lancelot as the lover of Queen Guenevere was well known in the fifteenth century, the effect of this is to introduce an element of romance, and reduce the unduly nationalistic tone, for Lancelot was a Frenchman. At the same time Malory maintained the historical and political relevance, for Professor Vinaver shows that there is good reason to suppose that Malory slightly recast Arthur's route in his expedition through France to accord better with that of King Henry V. In this section of Malory's work Arthur is probably to some extent an image of Henry V as in the alliterative poem he was of the equally heroic Edward III.

The 'prosification' of the alliterative *Morte*, though it appears as the second section of the Winchester MS and as Book V in Caxton,[6] may have been, as Vinaver argues, Malory's first 'work'. Although, as the reader already knows, the present writer does not agree with Professor Vinaver's further thesis that all the sections are entirely separate works, his view that the alliterative *Morte* was the first Arthurian section to be handled by Malory is an attractive one. It gives a sensible historical theory for the quality and success of Malory's work, showing fantasy grounded in historical relevance. It also helps us to grasp

[5] The Order of the Garter, founded by Edward III in the middle of the fourteenth century, is based on an Arthurian mythology.

[6] Caxton 'edited', that is, cut, this section more ruthlessly than any other, and undoubtedly here improved on Malory. See Shaw, in Bennett.

Malory's form. Malory did not, obviously, simply translate *Morte Arthure* through from beginning to end, or he would have come to Arthur's death before he had well begun. Yet the *Morte* gave two valuable leads to Malory. First, it is an example of a straightforward Arthurian story, enriched, certainly, by relevant digressions in the manner of medieval narration, but without the tiresome elaboration of interlacing. There were other examples of straightforward narration within or without a larger frame, but *Morte Arthure* was right in the centre of Malory's interest. The second lead is more complicated. *Morte Arthure* provides an example of medieval tragedy in the upward and downward movement of Fortune's Wheel, that great medieval image. Malory took the moment of triumph, but for the moment postponed the fall. His section on Arthur and the Roman Wars, taken from the alliterative *Morte*, does not, like the *Morte*, go on immediately to the discovery of Mordred's treachery and so to Arthur's return and death. Naturally, Malory knew that this was the end to which he would have to work, as a matter of history. But he wanted to dilate on the splendour of Arthur's achievement and on the achievements of Arthur's knights: here the romances, the mirror of chivalry, came to his aid. With their material Arthur's moment of triumph is prolonged, and we hear many adventures, including that of the Grail. Malory does not return to the alliterative *Morte Arthure* until he comes to the tragic end. The downward turn of Fortune's wheel is all the more tragic when we see the glory and complexity of what is destroyed.

When he comes to Arthur's end Malory does not use only the alliterative *Morte*. He has learnt to blend and select from various sources. So he uses a French source, and another English poem, the stanzaic *Morte Arthur*, to supply the material he works on.

The way Malory worked on his sources has been shown in fascinating detail by Professor Vinaver, and following him, by other scholars.[7] Briefly, Malory has selected from his sources those stories which he requires, thus 'breaking up', as Professor Vinaver has shown (*Works* p. lvii) 'the complicated structure' of the cyclic romances and 'using its fragments for smaller narrative patterns'. He makes '(a) a rearrangement of episodes consistent with [his] own narrative technique, and (b) a series of connecting passages designed to link together the episodes so rearranged' (*Works* p. 1575). Whereas Professor Vinaver sees the 'fragments' as entirely separate, it seems fair to say that most scholars now see the fragments arranged in the form of a larger whole (perhaps suggested by the alliterative *Morte*), which tells the whole life and death of Arthur and the marvellous deeds of his knights, with all that is implicit in them of romantic and historical significance.[8]

[7] See especially the work of Professor Lumiansky's team in Lumiansky (1).
[8] See my account in Bennett and see also Lumiansky (1) *passim*.

History (of a kind) and romance are now in Malory grown together. It is not literal historical truth for us, of course, since King Arthur never existed as Malory thought of him (though to many medieval Englishmen he did). It is not unreasonable, however, to think of Malory's feeling for England, for a special personal situation, for what creates and destroys great human institutions, as generally 'historical,' with a practical human relevance.

This human relevance feeds green sap through the romance of chivalric adventure and love; the events are no dry leaves of dream but living gleaming images of human life. Malory grafts on to the sturdy stock of *Morte Arthure* the exotic flowers of French romance, achieving the exchange and mutual enrichment of strength and beauty.

III

The Morte Darthur

The Morte Darthur is the name traditionally given to Malory's work, though, as the words of the colophon (see p. 158) presumably written by Malory suggest, the subject of the work is 'Arthur and his knights from the beginning to the ending'. Caxton first named it *The Morte Darthur*, though he noted that more was meant. The short title signifies the most important single event, which is certainly Arthur's death. Although Professor Vinaver concludes that the short title *The Morte Darthur* can apply only to the last of eight main parts, to which it literally belongs, practically the same title, *Morte Arthure*, had also been given in the fifteenth century manuscript to the whole alliterative poem which contains many other events. In the same way, *The Morte Darthur* covers the whole of Malory's book.

As will have been gathered from the discussion above, *The Morte Darthur* is a very long book, with many adventures intermingled. It cannot but contain some inconsistencies, though the effect of these is not disastrous. Most of them arise in the narrative of the adventures of knights in the middle section, when the Round Table is at the height of its glory. These adventures may be thought of as roughly parallel in the general time sequence. Such inconsistencies arise less obviously in the last two sections. A novelistic naturalism is, however, not to be expected, and the superficial resemblance of the book to a novel is misleading.

Nevertheless the book treats a coherent and cohesive mass of material, sorted with great care. The Arthurian stories had for long been known as 'the matter of Britain' (one of the three great topics of medieval romance), but for Malory, as for the author of *Morte Arthure*, the subject is not Britain but England. That Malory's chief hero, Lancelot, is French, only shows that

Malory's feeling is not a form of post-Renaissance xenophobia. The people and the vague localizations of the French sources are given an English local habitation which is named.[9] The castle of Meliagaunt is seven miles from Westminster. To get to it in a hurry, as Lancelot once had to, to rescue the Queen, you make your horse swim the Thames at Westminster, and land at Lambeth. Queen Guenevere, about to be married, goes up to London to buy her trousseau. Camelot is actually, Malory tells us, Winchester. Many other places are similarly identified. At another level Malory leaves no doubt of one of the themes that preoccupy him when he makes his well-known apostrophe to his fellow-Englishmen, reproaching them for their instability (p. 139). He fits Arthur's reign into what was known of pre-Anglo-Saxon chronology, and dates it in the fifth century. His interest in history is not ours; not impersonally political or economic, or social. His history was incarnate in the person of Arthur, and in Arthur's achievements and knights. Naturally it was real history-writing, a story, not annals.

The story is of the rise and fall of King Arthur, with which is closely involved the achievement and disaster of Lancelot, Arthur's principal knight, the strongest and bravest of all, who comes to a sad but pious end. The lives of the two are closely interwined, and their double thread holds all the great, varied, and beautiful tapestry together. Malory tells how Arthur is begotten, in a way that already plants the seeds of tragedy. He comes to the throne unknown, but chosen by fate and justified by his own bravery and honour. He establishes a great Empire, stretching from Ireland to Rome, and a brotherhood of warriors, the knights of the Round Table, whom he causes to be vowed to an ideal of equity, bravery, justice, help for the weak and oppressed, personal goodness. Many knights come to his court, attracted by the glory of the Round Table. From the court they depart on many strange adventures, returning to increase its glory. The strangest adventure of all is the search for the Holy Grail, symbol of healing for the Waste Land, to be attained only by the pure in heart. Three knights achieve it, notably Galahad, the son of Lancelot. Lancelot fails, for this adventure demands a perfection not given to even the best of ordinary mortals, and it is part of Malory's literary achievement that even Lancelot, 'the greatest knight of a sinful man', as Malory calls him, is yet so human. Lancelot comes nearer to achieving the Grail than any of the other 'ordinary' knights, but, strong and noble as he is, he is also proud and—by some standards—unstable. He is not unstable in the ordinary sense, because in his adulterous love for Arthur's Queen, Guenevere, he is all too stable; but unstable in his desire for moral perfection, as we all are. The signs of Lancelot's instability are his pride and his obsessive love for Arthur's Queen. Lancelot, after the Arthur of the earlier sections of the whole work, is the prime architect of the fame of Arthur's

[9] Cf. Stewart.

court. After his return from the Quest of the Holy Grail he is at the precarious height of his glory, the supreme ornament of that supreme institution, the Round Table. But the fine crack in the golden bowl of noble achievement that the Grail Quest has clearly revealed begins to widen. Because he loves Guenevere, and because he is honourable and loyal, Lancelot cannot desert her. Yet he cannot be the lover of Guenevere and remain honourable and loyal to Arthur. His pride must drive these honours and loyalties to destroy each other, and much else. Lancelot's own faults are emblematic of the evil that exists among some other of the knights. They are not necessarily adulterous, though many are incontinent; some are envious, others are vengeful (which are not faults of Lancelot), and some are proud. In a word, they are human. But the worst is Mordred, who is himself the illegitimate product of Arthur's own early sin, in his brief incestuous (though in this respect ignorant) affair with his half-sister. Mordred and others force the reluctant Arthur to recognize Lancelot and Guenevere's adultery; the lovers must abscond. Arthur must attack them; Mordred rebels in Arthur's absence and in the last battle mortally wounds him before dying himself at his own father's hand. The whole glorious and humanly insecure institution of chivalry, so briefly once achieved in that England where Malory later contemplated it with joy and sorrow, is brought crashing down. The death of the most noble knights of all the world, and the most noble king, is brought about by the faithful love of the best of them all. Had Lancelot been worse or better none of it would have happened. Arthur is carried off to the mysterious Avilion. Lancelot and Guenevere withdraw separately into lives of penitence and solitude until they die. Lancelot's soul goes to Heaven.

This is in briefest outline the story that Malory tells, or rather retells. It is the great secular story of Western medieval Christendom. Within the whole body of legend are found the grandest public themes and the dearest private concerns: the Great King and the Great Society; secret love and solitary death. Arthur himself is by turns, as the story develops and as he grows older, Hero, King, Father, finally destroyed by his son Mordred and surrogate-sons Gawain and Lancelot. They themselves are respectively villain, half-villain, hero. There is a whole range of motifs of the deepest antiquity, such as the modern conscious mind may barely recognize, of hope and doom, strange sicknesses, mysterious healing, enchantments, quests and journeys, conflicts, fatal or lucky chances. They are gathered together from the Celtic, Classical, Eastern past, mingled with and transformed by the Christian thought and passion of many different centuries. Malory welded them together in the image of England; his sober treatment of what was once wildest fancy reflects a political, military, historical concern. He is rationalistic in his cutting down of marvels, in his refusal of folk superstition. He is realistic in his estimate of what a man may do. He loves and admits high ideals and strange marvels, but cautiously, and after testing, so that they appear the more noble and marvellous. He senses both the development of a new individualism, and a new concept of the nation-state as a great institution, and finds in the clash between them some part of his tragic structure.

He does not think in terms of mass society, or of jingoism. He thinks of the brightness and eclipse of the ideal yet corrupted society that he imagined as Arthur's English court; of the glory and corruption of good men, in particular of those two aboundingly good men, Arthur and Lancelot, but also of some few intimates like Gawain and his brothers, and some few dozen more whose adventures brought them to the court, and who made up the noble fellowship of the Round Table. Specific as it was, localized in time and place, vivid, *there*, nevertheless Malory also created in his work an image, a model, that may be widely applied throughout one's own experience, and throughout our knowledge of human society in any country. Malory's book is about an ideal society, and its fall; good men and their faults; an exciting way of life, and a great tragedy.

Like all great authors his inclusiveness is such that he seems to us to be balanced at a significant point between past and present, and to hold together elements naturally in tension—the individual and society, passion and faithfulness, honour and sanctity, glory and shame. Even in form and structure he achieves an astonishing blend of the medieval and modern: his work has elements that relate it to the old cyclic romances, to modern short story and novel, to *The Faerie Queene*, even to Proust's great work; yet it maintains its own distinctive form, both between and of different worlds.

IV

THE STYLE OF A GENTLEMAN

Malory's style is supremely well suited to his matter; it is both colloquial and ceremonious—the style of a fifteenth century gentleman. He is not scholarly, genteel, nor boorish.[10] He is at one with Shakespeare's courtly Hotspur, who

[10] Malory's style has been regrettably little investigated. H. C. Wyld in what he describes as his 'lighthearted' *History* neglects Malory but for a few words of general praise. He points out, however, the colloquial yet ceremonious speech of gentry from the fifteenth to eighteenth centuries, and emphasises the close relation between the written and spoken word. Jan Simko, in the most elaborate, but still limited, treatment of Malory's language so far available finds in Malory's style the 'earthiness of popular speech,' contrasting with him Caxton's 'tradesman's' anxiety about 'correctness.' See also *Works* p. 1653.

required his wife to swear 'a good mouth-filling oath' 'like a lady'; with the ceremonious Lord Chesterfield, who thought it extremely rude to answer yes or no, without adding Sir, My Lord, Madam, according to the quality of the person addressed; and with the aristocratic Lord Byron.[11]

The colloquial vigour—there is no need to call it popular, if this implies what is non-aristocratic or non-gentrylike—is everywhere apparent. It appears in a blunt directness: Sir Lancelot 'sank down upon his arse' (p. 55) according to the Winchester MS; Caxton has 'buttocks', a more genteel middle-class word. Caxton's version is here not likely to be Malory's (see Note on the Text p. 37).

Not surprisingly, Malory comes out best with the spoken word of dialogue, vigorous, laconic, expressive. What richness of implication is rendered in Lancelot's sharp words to the queen. 'Have ye no doubt, madam, I allow your wit. It is of late come since ye were waxen so wise.' The restrained sarcasm tells a tale of personal relationships that Malory might have found it hard to put in more abstract, analytic terms—and which, had he done so, we should have found a good deal less interesting than its dramatic and concrete expression.

The colloquial energy of Malory's writing is particularly revealed by his syntax, which is plain enough, and rarely gives trouble, but which often has a fine unconcern for rules of proper relation, coordination, and subordination. He slides from clause to clause in a way that makes it difficult to impose modern bookish punctuation on his syntactic structures. Very often the interposed dash of a fluent letter-writer, did it not look typographically rather odd, would be the best punctuation to separate clause from clause. This sliding syntax is everywhere apparent, but most noticeably where Malory is writing on his own, unguided by the more formal French, as in the passage on May season (p. 100). Occasionally it degenerates into mere muddle (e.g. p. 150), where one feels that Malory must have been sleepy indeed; but more typically it occurs in the transitions between narrative, reported speech, and direct speech. Such a slide from one mode to another is not uncommon in Middle English generally, because Middle English writing is closer to colloquial speech than is most modern print, but in Malory it is especially frequent. It shows his confidence, his freedom from either social or scholarly anxieties; it is one of the ways in which his remarkable unity with diversity of tone is maintained.

The colloquial power of Malory's style cannot be properly estimated without recognizing what is a strange conjunction to the twentieth-century reader; the conjunction of the colloquial with the ceremonious. We tend to think that colloquial style is in every sense ruder and lower than other styles, and in its

[11] Cf. Wyld, pp. 17 ff., and Byron, *Don Juan* Canto XI, especially stanzas XLII–XLIV.

nature opposed to any form of high style. That is not the case with Chaucer[12], who was also a writer for the gentry and who could use a coarse word with courtliness; and it is not the case with Malory. Within the range of the spoken word and an unbookish diction his style easily comprehends a casual simplicity at one end of the scale and a deep-toned stateliness at the other. An obvious example of his style at its highest is Sir Ector's threnody for the dead Lancelot (p. 157). It rests on the simple use of a well-known rhetorical device, *anaphora* or *repetitio*, the repetition of an introductory phrase. This device had previously been very effectively used by Chaucer at the end of *Troilus*, at a similar point in the story, also summing up certain qualities of his hero, in the lines beginning 'Swich fyn . . .' (*Troilus* V 1828–32), with which Malory's passage may be usefully compared. Malory has less ambivalence, is more directly moving, and has his own complexity. He takes over the traditional paradoxical attributes of the Christian knight, his fierceness and gentleness, and by placing them in the mouth of a brother and faithful comrade gives them more expressive dramatic force of personal speech than could be obtained by direct author's comment. The use of the second person singular is also significantly moving, as will be later shown. Yet he does not aim at a realistic naturalism. The speech is not sobbed or gasped out, though we are told of the extremity of Sir Ector's grief. The speech has a liturgical solemnity, arising from a complex parallelism of phrase and idea that has its roots in the old alliterative poetry (see the notes), and possibly in biblical parallelism too. The speech is naturally at one extreme of Malory's stylistic range, just as bluntness of description, or Lancelot's sarcasm, is at the other. Between these extremes Malory modulates with extraordinary skill, keeping all the time an evenness of tone that is instantly recognizable. There is no disputing the sense of a living speech. ' "Fall whatsomever fall may", said sir Agravain,' or, as we now say, 'Come what may'. The words are entirely natural in their unforced expression of absolute determination. Living and natural as the colloquial tone is, it is not the clumsy inexpressive jargon of the downtrodden populace, deprived of so much of intellectual as of other riches. Malory may not have been an educated man in the way a clerk was educated, but he could and did read, like his own characters. His style was partly formed by the stateliness of the French prose with which he lived for what must have been many years. And he reflects the high manners of a society in which to speak well was itself one of the main expressions of good manners. There is a casual dignity of expression everywhere. Even in the amusing passage where Lancelot's own dignity is punctured by an arrow in the buttocks, Lancelot speaks with a crisp irritation that shows a delightfully gentlemanlike self-control in speaking to however errant a lady. Everywhere

[12] See my essay 'Chaucer and the English and European Traditions' in Brewer.

in the book the characters speak to each other in terms of ceremonious address—Sir, Madam, My Lord, My most redoubted king, Mine own lady, Fair maiden, Fair sister, and so forth.

The most striking example of Malory's language in its careful modulation of tones, revealing both its colloquial liveliness and ceremonious dignity, is to be found in his use of the second person of the personal pronoun. The normal pronoun of address is the second person plural, the polite, public form. It is almost always the form used between Lancelot and Guenevere. In their desperate plight when Agravain has trapped Lancelot in Guenevere's chamber, Lancelot still uses this polite, respectful form. Then, ' "Nay, sir Lancelot, nay!" said the queen, "Wit thou well that I will not live long after thy days." ' How moving is that brief change to the warmth and intimacy of the second person singular. Malory achieves a delicate effect here with minimal means. Guenevere immediately reverts to the plural and only once again does she use the second person singular to Lancelot, even more movingly, when she banishes him for ever: 'And therefore, sir Lancelot, I require thee and beseech thee heartily, for all the love that ever was betwixt us, that thou never see me no more in the visage. . . . ' And so the sad, tender, cruel words go on. Lancelot himself *never* uses the second person singular to her. There is much implicit here of their whole relationship and respective characters.[13]

Other uses of the second person singular as expressive of deep feeling, easily overlooked by a modern reader, but striking in themselves, are the rare occasions when Arthur uses it. The polite public plural form is almost always used by Arthur, even though he is always in the position of a superior addressing an inferior. Nothing points more clearly to his grace and courtesy as a king than this. But even Arthur breaks forth in sorrow and tenderness at Gawain's death-bed, 'Alas, sir Gawain, my sister son, here now thou liest, the man in

[13] For purposes of comparison it may be noted that in Chaucer's *Troilus and Criseyde* the lovers never use the second person singular to each other. In contrast, it is almost constantly used between the friends Troilus and Pandarus, though Pandarus has a tendency to use the second person plural at the beginning of a conversation with Troilus, presumably in acknowledgment of Troilus's superior social rank as a prince of the blood royal. One wonders indeed if there is not a shade of presumption in Pandarus's almost constant use of the singular form.

In the early fourteenth-century romance *Guy of Warwick*, probably intended for an audience less aristocratic than either Chaucer's or Malory's, the second person singular is very promiscuously used.

Caxton's text sometimes confuses *thou* and *ye*. The only place where the Winchester MS scribe seems wrong and Caxton right is on p. 137 where Caxton has the singular for the plural and the Winchester MS the reverse. I have corrected the text.

the world that I loved most;' and again, later, after the great defeat, ' "Ah, sir Lancelot", said king Arthur, "this day have I sore missed thee!" ' Almost as moving is his use of the second person singular to sir Bedivere, when Arthur is desperately near death, and must have Excalibur properly consigned to the lake, though the tenderness here becomes mixed with an imperious indignation which again is quite appropriately conveyed by the use of the singular form. His final words to Bedivere, harsh as they must be with the harshness of all inevitable partings, are nevertheless softened, made warm and human, by the use of the singular in the final request: 'in me is no trust for to trust in. . . . And if thou hear nevermore of me, pray for my soul.'

The note of intimate appeal is also marked by the fleeting use of the singular by sir Urry just before he is cured by sir Lancelot; and by Lancelot himself in his prayer, on the same occasion, where the intimacy of the address to God is not harmed by the accompanying formality—a mixture which, fossilized in the liturgy, is the only survival of the potency of the second person singular in English today. Lancelot also uses the singular form in brief prayer when trapped by Agravain.

The fullness of feeling which the singular form can convey in appropriate context reaches its effective climax in sir Ector's noble threnody for his brother and comrade, the hero of the whole book, with its repetition, both stately and intimate in a combination modern English can no longer match, of the second person singular itself; 'thou, sir Lancelot, there thou liest, thou were . . . thou were,' and the reiteration of 'thou were' eight times more. This is stylistically as bold as Lear's five times repeated 'never', though it has the additional weight of the peculiar mixture of feeling conveyed by the form itself.

There are other uses. Occasionally the singular form simply denotes the social superiority of the speaker to the person addressed, though there may also be a touch of other feeling present, such as anxiety or a sense of haste. Examples are Queen Guenevere's speech to the child who serves her, and whom she sends to Lancelot for rescue when Meliagaunt captures her; and Lancelot's own speech to the carter whom he asks for a lift to Meliagaunt's castle. This note of superiority is different from that of intimacy; the duality is of course perfectly familiar in second person singular usages in other European languages, though democratic levelling has removed it from English. The sometimes implied superiority, as well as the expressiveness, is essential for that other—again well-recognised use—of the singular form, as insult. To take Lancelot's adventures on the way to the castle of Meliagaunt again as an example, when he meets the archers he of course uses the plural form since there are more than one of them. But they add to the injury they do his horse the insult of using the singular form to him. It is insulting because they are socially inferior and also strangers. The first carter is similarly rude in using the singular form, being also one of Meliagaunt's men. But when Lancelot has struck him dead, the second carter is very careful to use the second person plural! When Lancelot arrives at Meliagaunt's castle he storms in with angry insult, calling on Meliagaunt, '*Thou* false traitor'.

The modulations from the polite and dignified plural to the insulting singular can be followed in the relationships between Lancelot and Gawain, after Lancelot has so unhappily killed Gawain's brother Gareth. Gawain constantly uses the insulting singular. Lancelot, with noble forbearance, with a grievous sense of his own fault, and of Gawain's partial justification, normally uses the plural form, but now and again is so sorely tried that he replies in the singular. When Gawain, after his wound, loses his hatred of Lancelot, he begins to use the plural form.

There is another interesting set of contrasts in the scene where Agravain and Mordred trap Lancelot with the Queen. In insulting excited triumph Agravain constantly uses the singular form. Lancelot, calm, courtly, determined, grim, is never shaken out of his self-control: he always uses the plural.

Whether Malory was self-conscious in his use of the various grammatical forms it is impossible—and unimportant—to know. The subtlety of their use is there, part of the structure of the book, and no reader will wish to remain insensitive to it. It is indicative of many other subtleties still insufficiently realised which this essay can only touch on. Some of them may be summed up in pointing to the dramatic terseness that also characterises Malory's style, indicative of a certain practical, man-of-the-world's tone, of a desire to get on with the story, and an English gentleman's feeling that he does not need to underline the effects and significance of his words. The social and personal insight conveyed by the varying use of a simple grammatical form can be matched in a hundred brief speeches where our alertness is rewarded by a richness and a sophistication that would not shame Chaucer, though it has been unaccountably overlooked by critics. A single brief example must serve here. When sir Gawain seeks the knight of the red sleeve who had done so well at the tournament (and who is Lancelot *incognito*) he eventually comes to the house of sir Bernard, the father of the fair maiden of Astolat, where Lancelot had stayed. Sir Bernard had lent Lancelot the shield of his sick son, sir Tirry, and sir Bernard's daughter, as she calmly and openly says, had fallen irrevocably in love with Lancelot. Gawain politely questions sir Bernard and his daughter about the identity of the unknown hero, who had left his own shield with them.

'Ah, fair damsel,' said sir Gawain, 'please it you to let me have a sight of that shield?' 'Sir,' she said, 'it is in my chamber, covered with a case, and if ye will come with me ye shall see it.' 'Not so,' said sir Bernard to his daughter, 'but send ye for that shield.'

The innocence and goodness of the girl could hardly be made more delight-fully plain. They are the basis of her honesty in love, and of the pathos of her fate. At the same time the entirely proper, sharp, worldly caution of her father removes any touch of sentimentality. The realism of the little scene extends from the 'shield in the case' to the intangibilities of character. The presumed French source is a long way away: it includes an otiose scene in which the promiscuous Gawain attempts to make love to the maiden, who repulses him. Gawain is a better man than this in Malory's last two main sections. The stanzaic English poem which also partly serves as source is equally remote from Malory; while not making Gawain so amorous the poem interestingly allows the maiden 'hend and fre' to take Gawain to her chamber to show him Lancelot's armour, left with her. Malory's worldly wit and wisdom, his sense of character and feeling, are in this, as in so many other places, enormously superior to, and really quite different from, his sources, whatever hints he may have received from them.

The terse dramatic realism of Malory's style, with its economic presentation of the essence of character and action mainly through speech, though apparent everywhere, can be seen with extraordinary vividness in the scene where Lancelot and Guenevere are trapped by Agravain and his followers. One can measure Malory's quality by presenting him in comparison with and contrast to his sources: here one can also do it by considering an effective modern treatment of the same episode in T. H. White's *The Once and Future King* (1958). White's account is about three times the length of Malory's, though the most crucial part of the fighting is evaded. It is much more realistic in giving everyday details. Lancelot spends a page brushing Guenevere's graying hair! The dialogue is full of the meaningless colloquialisms of normal modern speech: 'well', 'it was nice', 'do you know', 'really', etc. Much more attention is paid to, or at least more words are spent on, psychological motivation, and on the explanation of underlying psychological forces in a generalizing language attributed (rather unconvincingly) to the characters themselves. It is a touching and enjoyable scene completely and very competently in the manner of the conventional modern novel.

By contrast, Malory has no love-chat, no cosy domesticity. He deliberately refrains from prying into what the lovers were about—the physical details are not his interest; he knows what physical life is like, and assumes a similarly cool attitude in his readers. His dialogue reflects the essential attitudes and actions of the characters, and gives necessary information. It is not skimped, but not a word is wasted in the interests of a superficial verisimilitude. He notes physical actions as they reflect the essential situation; for example, 'Then he took the Queen in his arms and kissed her.' The fighting is not only stirring, it is technically quite convincing, granted Lancelot's strength, partly because

Malory does not, like White, deprive Lancelot of even a sword to start with. In a word, where realistic detail is *really* needed, Malory can select and present more artistically and more convincingly. (In general, Malory's realistic touches show his sense of practical necessity, as in the occasional references to money and treasure, which Professor Vinaver comments on rather scornfully (*Works* p. xxii).)

The picture that this selective drawing presents is remarkably full. Guenevere shows herself passionate, loving, selfish, cool, and entirely convincing—here, as elsewhere, the most fascinating, exasperating, and human of all medieval heroines. Lancelot similarly reveals himself in all his magnificence, unshakable and splendid in love or battle, noble yet disingenuous, proud and adulterous, yet never failing in courtesy, and with a simple piety. Economy and pace are never sacrificed to realism and ceremonious manners.

The comparison with T. H. White is not intended to denigrate his remarkable though lesser achievement, but to emphasise Malory's strength. The realism of conventional novelistic technique forces White into various kinds of triviality. Malory, though realistic, escapes trivial realism and constantly uses what White himself calls, but can only occasionally use, the High Language. There is an exalted tone in Malory's style, which reflects, no doubt, the true quality of his imagination as it rises to meet the greatness of his story. It would be a mistake to equate Malory's High Language only with the ceremoniousness I have already noted (though ceremony is an essential part of the High Language) if the emphasis on ceremony were to deny the poetic force also deriving from what is colloquial and direct and simple. Malory's supreme art lies in this, that his High Language, the poetic force of his style, is made up of his whole range of tone, and is as much simple as ceremonious. Similarly, his art moulds into a whole the other paradoxical compounds of violence and tenderness, worldliness and piety, realism and romance. All is held together in a style that springs from a culture and a literary imagination that in its rhythms could maintain these opposites in balance, in fruitful conjunction; a culture in which, despite Malory's own fears, the centre *could* hold. Rhythm is the most potent, least analysable, quality of literary style. We feel it on our pulses. We sense the living passionate voice in Malory's powerful, masculine movement; we respond to a deep (if narrow) sensibility and to an unshaken nerve: we are moved by the noble style of Malory's mind, that with unselfconscious dignity looks around his beleaguered world to save what he can. This is the style of Malory; the style of a gentleman.

V

STRUCTURE

The steady progressive movement of the style in detail is reflected in the general sequential line of the book as a whole, though sequence is less marked in the middle of *The Morte Darthur*, not given here, than in the final movement. From the end of the Grail story the narrative moves firmly onwards in a clear line, with certain constant preoccupations. We feel the compulsions of progressive cause and effect, while gradually the possibilities of choice before Lancelot and Guenevere narrow, as previous decisions begin to realize their inevitable effects.

The clear narrative development does not sacrifice richness to clarity. Although there is no interlacing, the narrative weaves its own pattern. The development of significant pattern may be most easily demonstrated in the series of stories leading to the first great crisis, when Guenevere and Lancelot abscond. In each story the recurrent main motif in the pattern is their love: next is their almost equally constant discordance, due to Guenevere's jealousy. Another motif is Lancelot's tendency (who can blame him?) to disappear. In all three stories misfortune comes to Guenevere, who is rescued at the last minute by Lancelot. (The first of these stories, *The Poisoned Apple*, is omitted from the present edition because of lack of space.) The stories, though significantly similar in outline, are not repetitious. They describe a relationship and its development, showing both nobility and the progression of guilt. In the first story, *The Poisoned Apple*, both Guenevere and Lancelot are entirely innocent, but they are shown to live in a dangerous environment. Then Lancelot's lovable greatness and goodness in so many ways is emphasised in the beautiful and touching story that follows, *The Fair Maid of Astolat*, which also shows us more of Guenevere, and which is completed by Lancelot's success in the Great Tournament. There follows in due sequence Guenevere's second dangerous adventure, this time her capture by Meliagaunt in the story entitled *The Knight of the Cart*. During this adventure she and Lancelot become morally in the wrong, though Lancelot when he fights Meliagaunt is technically in the right. (The advantages he gives Meliagaunt are further subtleties in favour of Lancelot.) Then again follows a brief episode to the greater glory of Lancelot —*The Healing of Sir Urry*, in which Malory, with his long lists (partly omitted in the present text), gathers up, as it were, all the glory of the Round Table, and sets Lancelot—whom we have recently seen to be now compromising his own integrity—at the peak of his glory. Lancelot weeps after his miraculous cure of Sir Urry; surely at the thought of what he might have been. It is a wonderful climactic stroke of characterization. Then we move into the eighth part of the whole book with no sense of discontinuity as we come to the third episode of Guenevere's danger, after she and Lancelot have been caught together in her room, where it is now clear that the chivalric convention that right is might has been reversed by Lancelot. Guenevere and Lancelot are known to be guilty, but Lancelot is prepared to brazen it out by fighting any one who speaks of their guilt. Right is no longer might. Might bewilderedly asserts that it is right. The appearance of honesty fails to correspond with reality. Ultimately reality will break through, to the destruction of all. Meanwhile Lancelot for the third and final time comes at the last minute to rescue the Queen, and in the mêlée kills the unarmed Gareth. The death of Gareth initiates another chain of ironic cause and effect, for it is specifically Gareth's death which arouses his brother Gawain's unrelenting hostility to Lancelot, which in its turn drives Arthur on against Lancelot in the next series of episodes.

The killing of Gareth is thus a bridge. Malory has carefully prepared it. In the episode of the Great Tournament, which rounds off the story of *The Fair Maid of Astolat*, Malory had strongly emphasized the goodness of Gareth and his devotion to Lancelot, as well as Lancelot's love for him. The nature of Malory's artistic concern to make connexions and build up cumulative patterns is plainly seen here.

What is even more clear is how Malory can use one event to achieve multiple effects. Implicit in our knowledge of Gareth is the whole of his past history, related in the fourth main section of the whole book with notable prominence. From that section the charm and endeavour of the unknown knight, his successful adventures, his love for and marriage to the lady whom he rescued, and especially Lancelot's knighting of him, are remembered, if only vaguely. That Lancelot should inadvertently kill Gareth is thus in itself one of Malory's most effective and painful ironies. It is also fraught with heavy consequences, symbolic of the internal destructiveness which causes the final collapse of Arthur's court. It is part of a long sequence of events which are related to each other and which build up patterns of event, theme, and underlying concept. The distinguishing mark of Malory's narrative in this respect is its sequaciousness, its connectedness. One sentence leads to the next, one event to the next. There is in almost every case even an explicit verbal connexion between the eight major sections of the whole book.[14] This connected narrative sequence weaves patterns whose effects come from events which are held in memory by the reader, and which thus interact as it were out of time. The patterns of event, character, theme, with the implicit concepts of loyalty, love, bravery and the rest, act over the whole book. Mordred, who is active in the last two main sections, is begotten by Arthur in the first main section. The three principal characters of the whole book, Arthur, Guenevere, Lancelot, are

[14] For proof see Brewer in Bennett.

all introduced in the first main section and are active throughout. The ethical ideal, the High Order of Knighthood, is instituted in the first section and is an implicit basis for all that later occurs. It has been said above that it is Malory's purpose to chronicle this ideal, as embodied in Arthur and his knights and as grounded in English history, in its rise, its glory and its fall, on Fortune's wheel, through the procession of time. A note at the end of this introduction sets out the structure of that chronicle schematically, as it is shown in the eight main parts. In that scheme, and in the various continuities of event, character, tone and underlying preoccupations, we may legitimately seek and find the 'unity' of structure in Malory's whole book.

At the same time we should not force our sense of unity. When a reader first comes to Malory's work, besides recognizing it as one mass, he also sees something that may be likened to the forest of pinnacles, spires and towers that rise within the walls of a medieval city. They are all in the one city—but what a bewildering variety! A few tower above the rest, are easily recognized, and are most important. Some are in obvious relationship to each other—a west-end tower to a central spire, a row of pinnacles leading along a great nave to another steeple. But there are many others. We reach them from the central square, but there is a bewildering complexity and many a tall building of ancient date seems only where it is because it is. There are stories in Malory's whole book which give one the same impression. They are there because they are there. They contribute to the variety, the richness, the interest, the pleasure; they are part of the general style and content of the book, as an old building is part of a town, but no one could claim they are part of an *organic* unity. How such an accumulation could come about has been explained above. Here the nineteenth-century concepts of 'organic unity' can only mislead. The whole book is the work of one man, but he has worked on the diverse material of many other men in various ages. Different points of view have been included with different stories. Some of the unity of the book is no more than the product of its history, a matter of mere incorporation of an interesting adventure. In this respect the narrative is like a circumambulation of the walls of a city, enclosing a variety of dwellings, as the walls of Chester or York enclose buildings of every date from Rome to the present day, yet still make one medieval city.

It must be insisted that medieval writers—and I include Shakespeare as well as Anglo-Saxon writers—tolerated a degree of inconsistency, of multiplicity of points of view, within one piece of writing, that the artistic totalitarianism of the twentieth-century finds hard to bear.[15] This does not mean that there is

[15] Cf. G. Shepherd in Stanley, pp. 10-11, 14-15, for Anglo-Saxon poetry; Mrs E. Salter considers that 'Chaucer could never have intended (*Troilus*) to be seen as a unified whole,' Lawlor, p. 106. The inconsistencies within Shakespeare's plays are self-evident, though critics sometimes waste time trying to

no general cohesion in the subject-matter, overriding, or at least not totally denied by, the separate constituents, especially in the last two main sections of *The Morte Darthur*. In such literature it will be found that one principal event, usually near the end of the work, effectively dominates the heterogeneous material. In the Bible it is the Crucifixion and Resurrection. In *Troilus* it is Criseyde's betrayal of the hero. With Malory it is the death of Arthur, with all that that implies of the tragedy of the honourable society he had created.

VI

The Tragedy of the Honourable Society

The main events of Malory's story he cannot alter. They are his 'matter'. But the interpretation of matter, the finer points of character, the general ethos, which in medieval French literary terminology were summed up as *sens*, the 'sense', are mainly his, as Professor Vinaver has shown.[16] Malory has his own view of the characters and often modifies the material supplied by his sources. A clear example of his independence in the present selection is the character of Gawain.[17] In the earliest chronicle versions, and in later works based on them, Gawain is Arthur's chief knight. He was displaced by Lancelot in the twelfth-century French versions, and being described in these versions as of an amorous, promiscuous nature, was presented in an unfavourable light by the Grail authors, with their ideal of the monk's life of chastity. Malory accepts Lancelot's predominance, but presents a Gawain of some complexity in the last two main sections. He is bold but not amorous; somewhat ambivalent in his attitude to Lancelot, yet not against him until the unfortunate killing of Gareth. He is then shown as angry and vengeful, inspired not only by love of Gareth but by the spirit of ancient family feud. At his death he repents. He is a simple, stubborn man, an outstanding fighter, formidable in his depth of feeling, passionately proud and fierce in his personal and family honour. There

---

explain them away. The Bible as one book is the great example of contained discontinuities, and such containment is characteristic of many separate books of the Bible as well. Cf. D. E. Nineham, *Saint Mark*, The Pelican Gospel Commentaries, 1963, especially pp. 29-30, for comments pertinent to the literary problem. Benson's valuable article on apparent inconsistency and tragedy in the alliterative *Morte Arthure* came to hand too late to be fully used, but supports what is argued here.

[16] *Works*, pp. lx ff.   [17] Cf. Whiting.

is nothing in him of the light-of-love, and Malory, as already noted, omits, for example, the French Gawain's genial attempt to seduce the Fair Maid of Astolat. Malory inevitably relies on his sources for most of his material, but never hesitates to take what he wants, to add, and to reject. He then presents the character economically and dramatically almost entirely through event and speech.

The other characters, even minor ones, have a similar solidity. How clearly, for example, is Meliagaunt's slippery nature presented; and yet we feel his genuine love for the Queen. How clearly the admirable 'steadfast Bors'[18] comes through; brave, loyal, sensible, stolid.

How subtle is the presentation of Arthur, the wise king, with his touch of irritable weariness, with his constant concern to hold together his great creation, his good society. If there are uncertaintities in our knowledge of his character it is because Malory has deliberately left them so. Similarly with Guenevere, so variable, always uneasy and jealous in her love for Lancelot, querulous and queenly. We catch a glimpse into her heart at times; at others, as with people we know in actuality, what she feels is a mystery; her speech is what she is. Exasperating in her imperious vagaries, she is perhaps victim as much as queen in a man's world.

When considering the variety and success of Malory's characterization one must also recognize that characterization *as such* is not his aim. The event has come first; the character's plausible speech comes next, as part of the interpretation, the *sens*. The interpretation itself is necessarily part of some general views or concepts implicit in the book. Malory himself rarely generalizes, and when he does it is but a brief passing comment, not itself to be taken at a very high level of generality. It would be mistaken, nevertheless, to think that his work did not have general implications.

Malory's presentation of love is clearly of great importance and has been well analysed recently by scholar-critics.[19] The love between Lancelot and Guenevere is represented as in itself good. When Lancelot and Guenevere are together, 'love that time was not as love nowadays'; that is, love was genuine, not merely lust. Malory says that he does not intend to discuss 'whether they were abed or at other manner of disports'. His French source says bluntly that they were in bed together. Malory is not avoiding such a plain statement because he is squeamish. Perhaps he is in part simply trying to palliate Lancelot's offence, and his later lies, but he is also making a point about their love's moral quality. Again, the whole episode of Elaine the Fair Maid of Astolat shows his sympathy with love and his open treatment of it. Elaine's innocence and goodness are in no way impaired because she openly confesses her love. Her dying

[18] Lumiansky (2).
[19] See P. E. Tucker in Bennett and R. T. Davies in Lawlor.

speech is Malory's own invention and he surely agrees with her refusal to obey the priest's command to forget sir Lancelot for whom she is dying, when she says, 'for my belief is that I do none offence, though I love an earthly man, unto God, for he formed me thereto, and all manner of good love cometh of God' (p. 68). That she would have had Lancelot even as a paramour, rather than not have him at all, does not bother Malory, or us. Malory's moral concern is deep but he is not a narrow moralist or moralizer. The same episode, along with others, shows that he has little interest in the elaborations of *fine amour*. It is honest faithful open love, in 'every lusty heart', with gentleness and service, that he approves of, as he says when talking about the month of May, which gives all lovers courage (p. 78). Again, love must be free; as Lancelot says, one cannot be constrained to love by egotistical demand. Yet love must be 'stable'. Gentleness, service, unselfishness, kindness, faithfulness (stability), all these are the distinguishing marks of true love, which is natural, formed in men and women by God, and so virtuous. Thus it is clear that Lancelot's love for Guenevere is in itself virtuous.

Lancelot's love is also criminal. Through the love that he and Guenevere loved together was the best fellowship of knights in the world destroyed. How can this be? For here is tragedy. To consider an answer we have to seek still deeper down among the general concepts that underlie *The Morte Darthur*, into concepts of honour and community, radical to the book, and indeed— like love—to our own lives.

Honour,[20] which Malory calls by its Old English name, 'worship,' still the usual word in his time, may be said to be the strongest single motivating force in the society which Malory creates. It is stronger even than love, even than Lancelot's love for the Queen: at least, when Bors and his friends advise Lancelot to rescue the Queen in her third and most dangerous predicament, it is to Lancelot's honour, and not his love, that they refer: 'it is more your worship that ye rescue the queen from this peril, insomuch that she hath it for your sake' (p. 108). Nor does Lancelot dispute this motive, though there is no doubt of his love.

How is honour obtained in this fierce, masculine, aristocratic society? Primarily, as numberless instances and remarks will show, by fighting bravely in battle or tournament; specifically, by defeating the enemy, or by helping friends who are in difficulty, and by fighting fairly. Secondarily, by associating with those who already have honour, especially, of course, with Arthur and Lancelot. Again, many incidents and more or less casual remarks anywhere in Malory make this plain. Presumably ladies' honour is also acquired by their association with honourable men. It clearly, as in Guenevere's case, need not

[20] For a very suggestive series of essays on this topic, in which the one by Professor Pitt-Rivers is especially relevant to Malory, see Peristiany.

derive from their chastity or marital faithfulness. It is however implicit that a
lady cannot associate with more than one or two men. But there are so few
women in this society, and they (even Guenevere) are so much at the disposal
of some man, that it is hard to generalize about them.

Honour demands certain personal loyalties. The first is to the king. The
second is to one's 'friends'. It is clear from the associates of Gawain and of
Lancelot, for example, that 'friends' include a kinship group, and another
different but overlapping group of those in a feudal relationship (perhaps
holding their lands in fee from the same lord). Also included among persons
to whom one must be loyal are those whom one has been helped by; but this
is not always an overriding obligation. Gawain has several times been helped
by Lancelot, yet becomes his enemy. That Gawain is nevertheless under such
obligation makes for deeper sadness and bitterness. Also included among
friends are those whom one has knighted or been knighted by. The particular
example in the present text is Gareth. That Lancelot should even accidentally
kill him whom he knighted is bitterly ironical; combined with the fact that
Gareth is Gawain's beloved brother, it further interweaves the tragic pattern.[21]
Finally, among friends bound by the obligations of honour are included those
who simply like each other. The outstanding practical example is Sir Lavain's
love for Lancelot, but the friendship between Lancelot and Gareth is another
important instance, while naturally brothers and feudal comrades may well
also love each other. Loyalty to the king and to friends should naturally
reinforce each other. It is part of the tragedy that these loyalties became
contradictory.

The third obligation of loyalty required by honour is toward the lady one
loves. In a good man such love is virtuous. Lancelot thus has a clear obligation
in honour towards Guenevere. In a true society the knight's loyalty to his lady
should coincide with loyalty towards king and friends, and again, a prime
element in the tragedy is the mutual incompatibility, for Lancelot, of his
loyalty to his king with that to his lady.

In honourable societies the deep question is the relationship between honour
and goodness. Professor Pitt-Rivers, in his important study, asserts that honour
and goodness are quite separate,[22] though society attempts to 'blur' the
distinction. In dealing with the problem Malory in *The Morte Darthur* is not
entirely clear: he has a rich inconsistency. But however one understands his
treatment there can be no doubt that one of the most powerful underlying
themes of the whole book, which is highly important in the culminating sections
of it presented here, is the relation between honour and goodness.

[21] The speech by Arthur on 'worship', significantly placed at the end of the
section 'The Great Tournament', is important.

[22] Peristiany, pp. 17, 30, 36

In the earlier parts of *The Morte Darthur* the identity of honour and goodness is assumed and the consequent behaviour incumbent on a knight is summed up in that ethical ideal, dear to Malory's heart, which he calls the High Order of Knighthood. It is expressed by the oath, mainly Malory's invention, which he tells us in the first main section that Arthur, having consolidated his kingdom and conquests, and having instituted his court of the Round Table, makes his knights swear every Pentecost:

> Then the king stablished all the knights and gave them that were of lands not rich, he gave them lands, and charged them never to do outrage nother murder, and always to flee treason, also by no mean to be cruel, but to give mercy unto him that asketh mercy, upon pain of forfeiture of their worship and lordship of king Arthur for evermore: and always to do ladies, damsels, and gentlewomen and widows succour; strength them in their rights, and never to enforce them upon pain of death. Also that no man take no battles in a wrongful quarrel for no love ne for no worlds goods. So unto this were all knights sworn of the Table Round, both old and young. And every year so were they sworn at the High Feast of Pentecost.

cf. Caxton Book IV, 15; *Works* pp. 119–20.
(Text constructed from Caxton and Winchester MS.)

This ideal of behaviour is an implicit standard throughout the whole book. When contemplating the actions described in the present selection the reader should have it constantly in mind, for Lancelot, for example, clearly engages in a wrongful quarrel for love. After making due allowance for the chivalric and literary conventions in which and through which the ideal is expressed it is clearly seen to be a noble and satisfying ideal of human behaviour; even within its conventions it is an excellent symbol for some of the most important concerns of all human life.

In the oath the association of honour with goodness is very close, for to do wrong is to forfeit honour ('worship'). There is another sanction, too: loss of the lordship of King Arthur; that is, in more modern terms, those who do wrong will be punished by ejection from society. The close association of honour with goodness is not the same as complete identification of the two. What honour and goodness here have in common is a reference to the same society, summed up as the 'lordship of King Arthur'.

The notion of fellowship, which, if it does not in Malory's work itself extend to a full concept of society, may at least be thought to symbolize society, deserves a little more emphasis. Its supreme exponent is of course King Arthur, whose constant care it is to foster his noble company of knights, and who in this surely has Malory's deepest sympathy. When Lancelot rescues the Queen from burning in the third of her misfortunes, and absconds with her, it is for the fellowship of knights of the Round Table, which is destroyed, that Arthur laments, and not for Guenevere. 'And therefore', said the king, 'wit you well, my heart was never so heavy as it is now. And much more I am sorrier for my good knights' loss than for the loss of my fair queen; for queens I might have enough, but such a fellowship of good knights shall never be togethers in no company' (p. 114). To take another example, the noble threnody for Lancelot's death spoken by Sir Ector (p. 157) expresses Lancelot's greatness, as much as anything in terms of social relationships. The comradeship that Malory feels so sympathetic towards is the pattern of a society that is, within its own conventions, confident, admirable, delightful, dynamic. It is composed of like-minded men, for the most part, and in it the individual can find both his friends and his own identity. Such a fellowship might well stand as a model for the supreme temporal, perhaps even the supreme eternal good, imaging a condition to which all social institutions and the men that make them might justly aspire. Malory expresses something of its successful achievement in his third, fourth and fifth main sections and its destruction is the theme of the seventh and eight sections as given here.

The tragedy has multiple causes; among them, Arthur's own fault in begetting Mordred, Mordred's and Agravain's malice, Lancelot's pride, his adultery with Guenevere, and so forth. Arthur himself may be thought to be at fault in that he is concerned so entirely with community, that is, with public virtues and necessities, that he neglects private virtues and necessities: that is, he fails to cherish his wife as an individual. Lancelot, on the other hand, is so concerned with his private obligations, in particular his obligation, which is clear, however immoral, towards Guenevere, that he denies public values.

Arthur's fault, if such it be, may be seen as a particular instance of a more general development which brings about the tragedy—the divergence of the values of honour and goodness from each other. The divergence is especially marked with Lancelot, for whom honour is the supreme value, as community is for Arthur. The clearest statement of the divergence of honour from goodness is made by Sir Bors when the queen is in peril of death because of the accusation of her adultery with Lancelot. Bors tells Lancelot he must

'knightly rescue her; for and ye did any other wise all the world would speak of you shame to the world's end. Insomuch as ye were taken with her, whether *ye did right other wrong*, it is now your part to hold with the queen.'

(p. 108)

Distinction between right and wrong must go when honour's at the stake. Thus an honourable man must sometimes tell lies.[23] Lancelot is justified by

[23] Cf. Pitt-Rivers in Peristiany, p. 32

honour in his various quibbles, prevarications and downright lies to preserve the Queen's good name ('name', or reputation, being a typical aspect of honour). Early in *The Morte Darthur* a maiden asks Lancelot for his love. He, the lover of Queen Guenevere, disclaims all interest in love. Critics have been puzzled. Is not this an inconsistency? No, it is a lie. Similarly, like an honourable gentleman, he lies to Arthur himself (p. 117).

Honour may permit, if it does not encourage, adultery or indeed promiscuous sexual intercourse. Lancelot is an adulterer, and Gawain, even in Malory, not chaste; but each is honourable. On the other hand, Lancelot considers he would be dishonourable if he were unfaithful to Guenevere, and he resists the attempt of Meliagaunt's damsel to seduce him. He can kiss and lose no worship, but nothing more (p. 91). Ladies also, if of high rank, may be honourable and unchaste: witness Guenevere and Iseult. Men of honour recognize this. Arthur, for example, is as prepared as King Mark to take back his wife after she has been living for some time with another man. But they must have an appearance of chastity; they must not be *spoken* of as unchaste.

A nice example of the difference between honour and virtue is the universal fact that a cuckold, but not an adulterer or seducer, is dishonoured. (There is an obvious biological force on the side of honour here, but that is true of other parts of honour, like physical prowess. For biology, might is right.) Arthur therefore is dishonoured as Lancelot is not by Lancelot's seduction of Guenevere (or by Guenevere's seduction of Lancelot). Gawain reminds Arthur of this. But to bring dishonour on the man to whom one owes loyalty is, if not dishonourable, at least ungrateful. That Lancelot clearly feels this makes his portrayal paradoxically more sympathetic.

If honour does not necessarily depend on virtue, it certainly depends on reputation, on what people *say*. Thus, although Guenevere's honour and shame (they are two sides of the same coin) do not depend on her chastity, they do depend on not being talked about. The importance of speech is clear in Bors' words quoted above. Honour's connexion with speech has given trouble to critics more virtuous or more simple-minded than Malory. For example, Malory keeps us in the dark about just how much Arthur knows of Guenevere's and Lancelot's adultery. The attempts by those excellent scholars Lumiansky and Moorman to work out in terms of novelistic realism how Arthur must have known all about it before the Grail Quest, how there must have been a reconciliation scene, and forgiveness, and a promise by Lancelot not to do it again, etc., are ingenious. They Bradleyize Malory, and *The Morte Darthur* is strong enough to stand the process. But the book is not a nineteenth-century novel, and such realism is beside the point, as Bradley's speculations about what goes on behind the scenes in Shakespeare's plays are often beside the point. So long as the lovers are reasonably discreet, and nobody *speaks* of them to

Arthur's face, he can remain apparently ignorant and need do nothing. Arthur is not a fool. He has a 'deeming' but he *does not want to know*. He was 'full loath that such a noise should be' (p. 102). Malory observes a similar honourable discretion. Honour and shame progressively throughout these final pages live more and more in men's mouths, less and less in relation to the actual state of affairs. Mordred forces Arthur's hand by witnessing Lancelot with Guenevere in her chamber and by telling Arthur so to his face. Malory shows us an Arthur very unwilling to have his hand forced. He knows Mordred is no friend to him. But once the 'noise', that is, the speech, is out, he is obliged by his own honour to act. Arthur has to say 'I may not with my worship but my queen must suffer death' (p. 110). It is one of Malory's subtleties and ironies that he here makes Gawain offer the king a way out by a lenient, though possible, interpretation of Lancelot's presence in Guenevere's chamber. But Arthur will not accept the way out, being for once, apparently, moved by a purely personal emotion, his 'ire' (p. 110). He asserts that Guenevere shall 'have the law' and be burnt. (Legality offers yet another structure within society, not necessarily coinciding with the structure of honour and virtue. Malory is not much interested in law, however—not surprisingly if our author is the Malory of Newbold Revel!—and we need not pursue it further here. Later on the king is ready to take Guenevere back and forget about the law.)

Arthur is the man of greatest honour in the kingdom[24] (p. 94), and here his honour puts him in a cruel position. But apart from personal anger he also invokes the law and by implication virtue as coincidental with his honour. We see once again here that Arthur's function is to draw together the various systems into one fellowship, with which he equates his honour. We may say that for Arthur, and perhaps for Malory, true honour coincides with virtue and law, and all together constitute the supreme value of fellowship. The story shows how fallen humanity fails to reach, or at any rate, to maintain, the ideal; 'things fall apart, the centre cannot hold'. Fellowship breaks, honour, virtue, law, separate themselves from each other. Honour becomes selfish, virtue corrupt, and law is set aside. When the honourable are not good, and when law becomes an instrument of revenge, when loyalties clash and good men are at odds, then treachery flourishes. The bonds of society fall apart and chaos is come again. It has happened often enough since the fifteenth century for us to be compelled by Malory's fifteenth-century symbol.

By a tragic paradox, that honour which has created the good society brings about its collapse. Arthur's honour has created the High Order of Knighthood,

[24] Here Malory appears to disagree with Pitt-Rivers, who asserts that the king is above the honour-system. Probably the difference here lies between the medieval concept of kingship, represented by Malory, and the later concept represented in most of Pitt-Rivers's sources.

foundation stone of a potentially ideal society. The same honour forces him, once the adultery is public, to enforce public law by condemning his queen to be burnt at the stake. Lancelot's honour leads him to perform brave deeds and loyally to keep his personal obligations whatever the cost to himself. The same honour forces him to rescue the Queen, whose love was also the inspiration of his honour. His honourable love and his love of honour lead him to be disloyal to Arthur, and also to conflict with an aspect of 'worship' as presented in the Pentecostal Oath of the High Order of Knighthood—that he should take on no battles in a wrongful quarrel for no love. Yet although Lancelot grieves over his disloyalty to Arthur and its result in the destruction of the whole society, he hesitates only a little to do what in honour bound he feels he must. His fault is very great, but it is Malory's achievement that we never pause in our love and admiration for Lancelot, and that Lancelot himself always appears so noble. It is part of the tragedy that one so greatly endowed with physical and spiritual gifts, in no way perverted or corrupt, the chief support of the glory of Arthur's court, should also be the chief agent of its destruction; that honour should destroy the honourable society.

The Morte Darthur tells the story of a tragedy, and if modern definitions of tragedy cannot encompass it, so much the worse for their definitiveness. The tragedy is the complex of the success and failure of the Round Table, and particularly of Arthur and Lancelot. They are not individualized tragic heroes, any more than the whole book is the unique production of one individual. Just as the book expresses in some sort the mind of the whole grand medieval episode of Europe's social and political history, so the heroes express in themselves something of English and European ideals and destinies, public and private. It is not fanciful to hear, as we watch the collapse of Arthur's empire, the long, slow, menacing echoes, rarely completely silent in European ears, of the grinding disastrous fall of the Roman Empire, and indeed, through the power of literature, of other empires since the fifteenth century, gone down in a rumble of dust and suffering. In Europe we still know the horror of disorder and collapse.

Though *The Morte Darthur* tells the story of such significant tragedy, it does not stop there. Medieval authors (and we may include Shakespeare and most of his contemporaries with them) did not call down the curtain at the moment of disaster. Europe knows that some life and words continue even though empires fall. But no one who lives through disaster is unchanged. Arthur can only die, since all that he has lived for has gone, and Malory, with his aristocratic rationalism, will have no truck with the folk-superstition of his return. The tragedy for Arthur lies not in the moment of his death, but in what had led to it, as is the case with Shakespearean tragic heroes. Lancelot and Guenevere turn to 'perfection'. The outline of the story is in Malory's sources, both French and English, although much of the detail and emphasis is Malory's own. Here again we deal with something deep in the European mind, which is the result of many men's strivings, experience, and meditations.

Lancelot's and Guenevere's turning to perfection, to saintliness, is something more than the expression of profound regret for their sins. It is also a repudiation of their whole previous way of life. Here we stumble across a basic paradox —or inconsistency—of medieval Christianity, perhaps of all Christianity, possibly of all human existence. Put simply, the best is the enemy of the good. Yet we find it hard enough to be even ordinarily good. In terms of Malory's book, all the characters attempt to be ordinarily good Christians within the context of what is for them ordinary decent society. This is true even of Lancelot, who may be said to excel only within the context of 'ordinariness', because he has received greater gifts than anyone else. And so, when caught in Guenevere's chamber, he naturally and casually invokes the help of Jesus to get out, and we warmly sympathize with him. C. S. Lewis is surely wrong when he denies that the persons in this society are Christians because in the end they come to repent.[25] If those only are Christians who have nothing to repent, then Christians are few indeed. These knights are not saints, and have much to be sorry for, but that is true of nearly everyone. Yet it is right to see a different quality of life, a different standard and different point of view invoked when Lancelot, and Guenevere, and others, turn to penitence. Their saintliness repudiates not only their past vices but their past virtues too. Saintliness, as the anthropologists have observed, cuts wholly across the honourable society. There have been hints of this earlier in the story. For example, the hermit who looks after Lancelot in the story of The Fair Maid of Astolat was once a member of the Round Table, a knight of honour and prowess, but now being a hermit, vowed to God, he has consciously abandoned his loyalty to Arthur and the Round Table (p. 55). Again, much of Lancelot's own honour, and even his good deeds, arise from pride, as he himself confesses (for example, p. 155) and as was driven home to him in the adventure of the Grail. His worldly pride is source of both virtue and vice.

Lancelot's repudiation, in itself tragic in intensity, adds another light on the tragedy of the honourable society. His saintliness repudiates honour and shame, and substitutes for them the concepts of innocence and guilt, which are standards of goodness, not honour, and which are also, in our kind of society at least, expressions of an internalized, individual, set of values, held, if necessary, in utter unconformity with the crowd. The individualism that conceives of guilt, therefore, by that very conception may need to reject the whole notion of society, as Lancelot does by becoming a hermit, who is the expression of a pure, unsocial (but not anti-social) individualism.

[25] Lewis p. 1

Lancelot's destiny also shows, in Arthurian terms, how the Cistercian authors of the anti-chivalric story of the Grail finally achieved their end. The monkish otherworldly ideal overcomes, through sheer persistence, the moral and chivalric this-worldly ideal. Here we may well be reminded of the similar transcendent destiny of another great medieval hero, Chaucer's *Troilus*, who, after death, surveys and despises secular sufferings, and by implication his past way of life.

In this respect *The Morte Darthur* is, like the *Troilus*, as Professor Shepherd has well said,[26] a 'romance in a tragic mode'. The shift of the plane of narration at the end, the invocation of transcendent values, expresses that mysterious sense of destiny, of the total relativity of earthly life and of all our most passionately followed desires and even values, that is one of the great powers of medieval tragedy. Not merely have we agonized over the destruction of the honourable society: by a last twist of tragic irony we are told that we need not, so it *now* seems, have agonized at all. When we are young this is too bitter a tragic pill to swallow. The 'tears in things' are sweeter than this. But perhaps there are few who are middle-aged or more who cannot recognize some of their experience here; as if to say, in trivial mundane terms, 'I was miserable over nothing'. Still this is not all. The shift to transcendence can also suggest a sense of mysterious fate, the ineluctable process to an inescapable end, the abiding question of the ultimate values that surround life as well as penetrate it. None, or few, can nowadays accept the specific, historically conditioned formulation of the transcendent heavenly destiny of humanity as it appears in medieval fiction. But we *can* recognize the validity of the perceptions which underlie that formulation: and even if we do not believe in heaven we know that at least we shall shift from the plane of earthly existence: we shall die. Death is the mystery that surrounds all life. Medieval tragedy, not centred on the individual, contemplates instead the universal progress from life to death and the inevitable dualities in life that such contemplation reveals. It is useless to complain of inconsistency. Death is inconsistent with life.

Although Malory's work can properly sustain such generalizations it is typical of its layered richness that these are not the only reflections we are left with. Although Lancelot's fate impugns the very concept of the honourable society, the validity of the good chivalric fellowship on earth, Malory himself does not fully accept this. It is still possible for him at the very end to refer to 'worshipful' men with respect. The superb threnody spoken over Lancelot's dead body by Sir Ector exalts again in Lancelot the great European heroic ideal, found as early as *Beowulf*, the ideal of the knight fierce as a lion in the field, gentle as a lamb in the hall, which is reiterated throughout medieval

---

[26] Shepherd, in Brewer, p. 86

literature, and potent in the later, derived, concept of the gentleman.[27] This is a worldly, though noble, ideal. And paradoxically Lancelot's good end though in one way a condemnation of his earlier life, is also a validation of it. He was a good man in the appropriate circumstances of the various ages of man. Malory's contemporary, Sir Stephen Scrope, as Ferguson in his valuable book points out,[28] recommends in all serious actuality that when a knight becomes too old and feeble for earthly chivalry, he should take up spiritual chivalry, moral contemplation, and spiritual deeds. Shakespeare makes Prospero do much the same. Whatever one may think of the morality of this it is certainly human and—given the premises—sensible.

So we return once more to the relation of honour and goodness, to the maintenance of true fellowship. Arthur lives and dies by this ideal. Lancelot goes beyond it. All individual men, from kings to those peasants whom Malory so totally disregards, must in their individual selves go beyond it, to die alone. But at another level society continues, even through disaster. Perhaps this is one of the basic confidences of English and European society which the very absurdity of the pseudo-history of the Kings of Britain, especially as received in the fifteenth and sixteenth centuries, might be taken to illustrate. Even from Troy, through its fall, to rise in Rome, through *its* fall, to rise again, as Christendom in all its struggle and difficulties had risen; from far back, and through whatever setbacks, the faith in human fellowship continues. So it happened in fifteenth and sixteenth century England's transformation of difficulty into dynamism, through the efforts of many men who shared Malory's views, and no doubt in part through the effect of *The Morte Darthur* itself. The sense of *general* survival and continuity is strong in Shakespeare's tragedies, especially, of course, in *King Lear*. A good deal of this feeling has gone into English society, which has sought solidarity within itself, and successfully survived apparently overwhelming threats to its existence, for a good many centuries now. Something of such confidence comes at the end of *The Morte Darthur* when we are told that Constantine ruled this realm, England, 'worshipfully'. The honourable society must always, being human, collapse, and must always be left behind, and yet must always continue. Malory asserts the possibility that honour may be the same as goodness; that Christians may be good men, even if most of them do not want to be monks, and cannot be saints;[29] and by a fruitful paradox of inconsistency he asserts the validity of this worldly ideal

[27] It seems to be a European ideal. My very able Japanese students confronted with Chaucer's formulation of it in the description of the Knight in the General Prologue to *The Canterbury Tales* thought that Chaucer was being comic. The *samurai* were different.

[28] Ferguson, p. 56

[29] Cf. T. C. Rumble's interesting study in Lumiansky (1).

as well as of the transcendental ideal. He asserts, in fact, through and along with his tragedy, the possibility, and indeed the requirement, for English gentlemen, of living good lives here on earth in a good society. And this assertion is fully in accord with the sober rationalistic realistic temper of so much of his book. I express his assertion in local terms here, for obvious historical reasons. But everyone of good will, of whatever race and society, can see the symbol in his own terms, recognize its significance for his own ideals, take it to his own business and bosom.

VII

THE AUTHOR AND DATE OF
THE MORTE DARTHUR[30]

At the end of *The Morte Darthur* the author says he completed the work in the ninth year of the reign of Edward IV (i.e. between 4 March 1469 and 3 March 1470), names himself 'Thomas Maleore knyght', and asks his readers to pray for his deliverance, presumably from prison. In the Winchester Manuscript he makes the same request for deliverance at the end of *The Tale of Sir Gareth*, and at the end of *The Tale of King Arthur* he names himself again as a 'knyght presoner'. Records so far known appear to reveal only one knight-prisoner named Malory (which has several different spellings) between 1460 and 1470, though he seems to have had a somewhat surprising career. He was a gentleman of an old Warwickshire family who succeeded to his estate at Newbold Revel in Warwickshire in 1433 or 1434. He served at Calais in the train of the Earl of Warwick with one lance and two archers, and married some years later. Then in 1450 to 1451, when he was about forty or more, he was charged with several major crimes—robbery, theft, two cattle-raids, extortions, rape, attempted murder. He was imprisoned, escaped by swimming the moat, and is then alleged to have broken into and robbed an abbey, repeating the offence the next day. He was imprisoned from August 1451 to 1454, with a brief interval, and on release continued, it is alleged, offences such as cattle-raids, in Essex. He was gaoled in Colchester, then London. In 1455 he was pardoned; in 1456 he served as Member of Parliament for his shire. He had several spells in prison afterwards, in some cases perhaps for debt, but he was in the train of Edward IV when he went to Northumberland in November 1462, and with the Earl of Warwick at the siege of Alnwick in January 1463—

---

[30] In this summary account I follow *Works*, p. xiii *et seq.*; Vinaver; and Baugh. At the time of writing a publication by William Matthews apparently disputing the identification of the author with Malory of Newbold Revel has been announced but has not appeared.

which may account for the mention of Alnwick, and even of Bamborough (of which the siege was raised on Christmas Eve, 1462) in the last section of *The Morte Darthur* (p. 155 below). He was specifically excluded from two general pardons granted to members of the Lancastrian faction in 1468, and may have been in prison again. He died on 14 March 1471 and was buried near Newgate. The book, finished in 1469, must have occupied parts of the last decade or two of his life, from about forty to sixty, presumably when bouts of prison (of a gentlemanly kind, with books and paper, pen and ink allowed) gave him leisure to write. His work, especially the final parts, is the distillation of mature and varied experience.

His career is by no means necessarily that of a scoundrel. Leaving aside the point that allegations are not proof, and assuming that Malory did some things that may well have been like those he was charged with, one must also take into account the violent factionalism of the time of the Wars of the Roses. The Warwick interest supported now Yorkists, now Lancastrians, and some, perhaps most, of Malory's deeds may have been for him a warlike pillage, while the accusation may be similarly inspired. Cattle-raiding is not necessarily beneath a gentleman, as many a Highland chief could witness. Malory is accused of twice forcing Joan, the wife of Hugh Smith. Without wishing to palliate an evil crime, or traduce a dead woman's name, it might also be said that while to be forced once was misfortune, to be forced twice by the same man argues carelessness on someone's part—or some degree of affection. In a word, to parallel a remark made by C. S. Lewis, we might think differently even of Lancelot if the only evidence of his life that we possessed was the charges prepared by King Arthur's solicitors during the war.

The truth is that even if Malory of Newbold Revel was the author of *The Morte Darthur* we shall never know in any significant degree what kind of man he was: the aim of the above remarks is simply to show that it is not inconceivable that a man with such a record, however we interpret it, could have written such a book. The author of the book, we can have little doubt, was a gentleman, vital and passionate, of an intense, even obsessive imagination, who, no doubt, like almost everyone else in this world, behaved much less well than he ought to have done and probably than he wanted to do. It is all too possible to know the good and follow the bad: 'the evil that I would not, that I do'. Although there is a connexion between a man and his book it is indirect and obscure at the best of times. We have no real evidence for the personality of Malory the man, and are not likely to get it even if he turns out to be from somewhere else than Newbold Revel. And anyway, the man is dead. The book lives.

VIII

A Note on the Text

The text is based on the Winchester MS, which has been compared with Caxton's version as printed by H. O. Sommer. Much of this work has of course been done in Professor Vinaver's edition, but in a number of instances (many of them already suggested by Professor Vinaver) I have preferred Caxton's version against the Winchester MS, and against Professor Vinaver's text, as being more likely to represent Malory's intention. In the many cases where there are trivial variations between Caxton and Winchester, and Malory's original is impossible to decide, I have followed the Winchester version. I have signified with an asterisk any variation here from the Winchester MS as edited by Professor Vinaver in his Oxford Standard Authors edition, 1954, but as this present edition is not intended for textual critics I have not engaged in discussion of such matters.

The spelling is modernized as far as it can be without changing forms fundamentally. Punctuation, capitalization and paragraphing are editorial and though indebted to Professor Vinaver's lead in this as in other matters I have often differed from him.

Annotation is extremely light. There are very few difficulties in the text. The fascinating pursuit of Malory's sources, with the reflections it prompts on his aims and methods, is already made possible by Professor Vinaver's notes, and the work of other scholars. But fascinating as it is, that pursuit must be secondary to the enjoyment and interest of Malory's own text as it stands, to concentrate on which is the principal aim of this edition.

A Note on the Structure of 'The Morte Darthur'

The parts are those of the Winchester MS. The titles are essentially those conferred by Professor Vinaver in the Oxford Standard Authors Edition (cf. p. 37). Vinaver's subsections of Parts 7 and 8 only are given here. C= Caxton's edition.

Part I   *The Tale of King Arthur* (C 1–4)
          (Tells the story of Arthur's miraculous birth, his wars of establishment and his marriage to Guenevere.)

Part II   *Arthur the Emperor* (C 5)
          (Tells the story of the Roman War and introduces Lancelot as a great warrior.)

Part III   *Lancelot* (C 6)
          (Tells his adventures.)

Part IV   *Gareth* (C 7)
          (Tells his adventures and marriage.)

Part V   *Tristram* (C 8–12)
          (Tells the story of Tristram and Isolde, with many others intermingled. Towards the end is told how Lancelot is tricked into begetting Galahad.)

Part VI   *Sankgreall* (C 13–17)
          (Tells how Galahad becomes a member of the Round Table, and all the knights depart on the Quest of the Holy Grail. Galahad, accompanied by Perceval and Bors, achieves the Grail, but only Bors returns. Lancelot partially succeeds. The others fail.)

Part VII   *Lancelot and Guenevere* (C 18–19)
      1. The Poisoned Apple
      2. The Fair Maid of Astolat
      3. The Great Tournament
      4. The Knight of the Cart
      5. The Healing of Sir Urry

Part VIII   *The Morte Arthur* (C 20–1)
      1. Slander and Strife
      2. The Vengeance of Sir Gawain
      3. The Siege of Benwick
      4. The Day of Destiny
      5. The Dolorous Death and Departing out of this world of Sir Lancelot and Queen Guenevere

The whole book may be said to follow a roughly threefold movement. Movement I, composed of Parts I and II, shows Arthur's upward rise; Movement II, composed of Parts III, IV, V, shows the varied greatness of the knights of the Round Table and the peak of Arthur's glory; in Movement III the wheel of Fortune, starting at its height, goes on to its downward movement, showing the downfall of the Round Table and of Arthur, Lancelot and Guenevere.

Select Bibliography

Baugh	A. C. Baugh, 'Documenting Sir Thomas Malory,' *Speculum*, VIII (1933), 3–29 and *Journal of English and Germanic Philology*, XXIX (1930), 452–7.
Bennett	J. A. W. Bennett (ed.), *Essays on Malory*, London, 1963
Benson	L. D. Benson, 'The alliterative *Morte Arthure* and Medieval Tragedy', *Tennessee Studies in Literature*, XI (1966), 75–87
Bradbrook	M. Bradbrook, *Sir Thomas Malory*, London, 1958
Brewer	D. S. Brewer (ed.), *Chaucer and Chaucerians*, London, 1966
Caxton	Sir Thomas Malory *Morte Darthur* (ed. and pub. by Caxton), 1485
Chambers	E. K. Chambers, *Arthur of Britain*, London, 1927
Davies	R. T. Davies, 'The Worshipful Way in Malory', in Lawlor, 157–77
Donaldson	E. T. Donaldson, 'Malory and the Stanzaic *Le Morte Arthur*', *Studies in Philology*, XLVII (1950), 460–72
Ferguson	A. B. Ferguson, *The Indian Summer of English Chivalry*, Durham, N.C., 1960
Galfridus	Galfridus Monumetensis, *Historia Regum Britanniae*, ed. E. Faral, *La Légende Arthurienne*, Paris, 1929; and see next
Geoffrey	Geoffrey of Monmouth, *The History of the Kings of Britain*, translated with an introduction by Lewis Thorpe, Penguin Books, London, 1966
Lawlor	*Patterns of Love and Courtesy*, ed. J. Lawlor, London, 1966
Lewis	C. S. Lewis, *Studies in Medieval and Renaissance Literature*, Cambridge, 1966
Loomis (1)	R. S. Loomis, *The Development of Arthurian Romance*, London, 1963
Loomis (2)	*Arthurian Literature in the Middle Ages*, ed. R. S. Loomis, London, 1959 ·
Lumiansky (1)	*Malory's Originality*, ed. R. M. Lumiansky, Baltimore, 1964
Lumiansky (2)	R. M. Lumiansky, 'Malory's Steadfast Bors', *Texas Studies in English*, VIII (1958), 5–20
Miko	S. J. Miko, 'Malory and the Chivalric Order', *Medium Aevum*, XXV (1966), 211–30
Moorman	Charles Moorman, *The Book of King Arthur*, Kentucky, 1965
Morte Arthur	*Le Morte Arthur*, ed. J. D. Bruce, Early English Text Society, E. S. 88, London, 1903

Morte Arthure	*Morte Arthure*, ed. E. Brock, Early English Text Society, O.S. 8, London, 1871
Peristiany	*Honour and Shame. The Values of Mediterranean Society*, ed. J. G. Peristiany, London, 1966
Rumble	T. C. Rumble, ' "The Tale of Tristram": Development by Analogy,' in Lumiansky (1), 118–83
Salter	E. Salter, '*Troilus and Criseyde*: a Reconsideration', in Lawlor, 86–106
Shaw	Sally Shaw, 'Caxton and Malory', in Bennett, 114–45
Shepherd (1)	G. T. Shepherd, 'Troilus and Criseyde', in Brewer, 65–87
Shepherd (2)	G. T. Shepherd, 'Scriptural Poetry', in Stanley, 1–36
Simko	Jan Simko, *Word Order in the Winchester Manuscript and Caxton's Edition—a comparison*, Prague, 1957
Stanley	*Continuations and Beginnings*, ed. E. G. Stanley, London, 1966
Stewart	G. R. Stewart, 'English Geography in Malory's *Morte D'Arthur*', Modern Language Review, XXX (1935), 204–9
Tucker	P. E. Tucker, 'Chivalry in the *Morte*', in Bennett, 64–103
Vinaver	E. Vinaver, *Sir Thomas Malory*, London, 1929
White	T. H. White, *The Once and Future King*, London, 1958
Whiting	B. J. Whiting, 'Gawain: His Reputation, His Courtesy', Medieval Studies, IX (1947)
Works	*The Works of Sir Thomas Malory*, ed. E. Vinaver, 3 vols., London, 1947
Wyld	H. C. Wyld, *History of Modern Colloquial English*, 3rd ed., London, 1936

The following have appeared since this book went to press:

W. Matthews, *The Ill-framed Knight*, Berkeley and Los Angeles, 1966

Sir Thomas Malory, *King Arthur and his Knights*, ed. R. T. Davies, London, 1967

C. Moorman, *A Knyght There Was*, Lexington, 1967

S. Noguchi, "The Paradox of the Character of Malory's Language," *Hiroshima Studies in English Language and Literature*, XIII (1967), pp. 115–134

Too late to be noted in the first edition appeared the Second Edition of Malory's *Works*, ed. E. Vinaver, Oxford, 1967. Some comment on the new edition, on some more recent studies, and on the modern criticism of Malory will be found in my essay 'The Present Study of Malory' in *Forum for Modern Language Studies* VI (1970), 83–97, which will also be issued as *Arthurian Romance: Seven Essays*, ed. D. D. R. Owen, Scottish Academic Press, St. Andrews, Scotland, 1970.

Caxton's Preface

After that I had accomplished and finished divers histories as well of contemplation as of other historial and worldly acts of great conquerors and princes, and also certain books of ensamples and doctrine, many noble and divers gentlemen of this royame of England camen and demanded me many and ofttimes wherefore that I have not do made and enprint the noble history of the Saint Grail and of the most renowmed Christian king, first and chief of the three best Christian, and worthy, King Arthur, which ought most to be remembered among us Englishmen tofore all other Christian kings.

For it is notoirly known through the universal world that there been nine worthy and the best that ever were, that is to wit, three Paynims, three Jews, and three Christian men. As for the Paynims, they were tofore the Incarnation of Christ, which were named, the first, Hector of Troy, of whom th'history is comen both in ballad and in prose, the second Alexander the Great, and the third Julius Cæsar, Emperor of Rome, of whom th'histories been well known and had. And as for the three Jews which also were tofore th'Incarnation of our Lord, of whom the first was Duke Joshua which brought the children of Israel into the land of behest, the second David, king of Jerusalem, and the third Judas Maccabeus; of these three the Bible rehearseth all their noble histories and acts. And sith the said Incarnation have been three noble Christian men stalled and admitted through the universal world into the number of the nine best and worthy, of whom was first the noble Arthur, whose noble acts I purpose to write in this present book here following. The second was Charlemagne, or Charles the Great, of whom th'history is had in many places, both in French and English; and the third and last was Godfrey of Bologne, of whose acts and life I made a book unto th'excellent prince and king of noble memory, King Edward the Fourth.

The said noble gentlemen instantly required me t'emprint th' history of the said noble king and conqueror King Arthur and of his knights, with th'history of the Saint Grail and of the death and ending of the said Arthur, affirming that I ought rather t'enprint his acts and noble feats than of Godfrey of Bologne or any of the other eight, considering that he was a man born within this royame and king and emperor of the same, and that there been in French divers and many noble volumes of his acts, and also of his knights.

To whom I answered that divers men hold opinion that there was no such Arthur and that all such books as been made of him been but feigned and fables, because that some chronicles make of him no mention ne remember him nothing, ne of his knights.

Whereto they answered, and one in special said, that in him that should say or think that there was never such a king called Arthur might well be aretted great folly and blindness, for he said that there were many evidences of the contrary. First, ye may see his sepulture in the monastery of Glastonbury; and also in Polychronicon, in the fifth book, the sixth chapter, and in the seventh book, the twenty-third chapter, where his body was buried, and after founden and translated into the said monastery. Ye shall see also in th'history of Bochas, in his book DE CASU PRINCIPUM, part of his noble acts, and also of his fall. Also Galfridus, in his British book, recounteth his life. And in divers places of England many remembrances been yet of him and shall remain perpetually, and also of his knights: first, in the abbey of Westminster, at Saint Edward's shrine, remaineth the print of his seal in red wax, closed in beryl, in which is written PATRICIUS ARTHURUS BRITANNIE GALLIE GERMANIE DACIE IMPERATOR; item, in the castle of Dover ye may see Gawain's skull and Cradok's mantle; at Winchester the Round Table; in other places Launcelot's sword and many other things.

Then, all these things considered, there can no man reasonably gainsay but there was a king of this land named Arthur. For in all places, Christian and heathen, he is reputed and taken for one of the nine worthy, and the first of the three Christian men. And also he is more spoken of beyond the sea, mo books made of his noble acts, than there be in England; as well in Dutch, Italian, Spanish, and Greekish, as in French. And yet of record remain in witness of him in Wales, in the town of Camelot, the great stones and marvellous works of iron lying under the ground, and royal vaults, which divers now living hath seen. Wherefore it is a marvel why he is no more renowmed in his own country, save only it accordeth to the word of God, which saith that no man is accept for a prophet in his own country.

Then, all these things foresaid alleged, I could not well deny but that there was such a noble king named Arthur, and reputed one of the nine worthy, and first and chief of the Christian men. And many noble volumes be made of him and of his noble knights in French, which I have seen and read beyond the sea, which been not had in our maternal tongue. But in Welsh been many, and also in French, and some in English, but nowhere nigh all. Wherefore, such as have late been drawn out briefly into English, I have, after the simple cunning that God hath sent to me, under the favour and correction of all noble lords and gentlemen, enprised to enprint a book of the noble histories of the said King Arthur and of certain of his knights, after a copy unto me delivered, which copy Sir Thomas Malory did take out of certain books of French and reduced it into English.

And I, according to my copy, have done set it in enprint to the intent that noble men may see and learn the noble acts of chivalry, the gentle and virtuous deeds that some knights used in tho days, by which they came to honour, and how they that were vicious were punished and oft put to shame and rebuke; humbly beseeching all noble lords and ladies with all other estates, of what estate or degree they been of, that shall see and read in this said book and work, that they take the good and honest acts in their remembrance, and to follow the same; wherein they shall find many joyous and pleasant histories and noble and renowmed acts of humanity, gentleness, and chivalries. For herein may be seen noble chivalry, courtesy, humanity, friendliness, hardiness, love, friendship, cowardice, murder, hate, virtue and sin. Do after the good and leave the evil, and it shall bring you to good fame and renommé.

And for to pass the time this book shall be pleasant to read in, but for to give faith and believe that all is true that is contained herein, ye be at your liberty. But all is written for our doctrine, and for to beware that we fall not to vice ne sin, but t'exercise and follow virtue, by which we may come and attain to good fame and renommé in this life, and after this short and transitory life to come unto everlasting bliss in heaven; the which He grant us that reigneth in heaven, the Blessed Trinity. AMEN.

Then, to proceed forth in this said book, which I direct unto all noble princes, lords, and ladies, gentlemen or gentlewomen, that desire to read or hear read of the noble and joyous history of the great conqueror and excellent king, King Arthur, sometime king of this noble royame then called Britain, I, William Caxton, simple person, present this book following which I have enprised t'enprint: and treateth of the noble acts, feats of arms of chivalry, prowess, hardiness, humanity, love, courtesy, and very gentleness, with many wonderful histories and adventures.

(*Caxton then proceeds briefly to summarize the contents divided into twenty-one books*)

THE MORTE DARTHUR
PART SEVEN

Lancelot and Guenevere

1. The Poisoned Apple

So after the quest of the Sankgreall was fulfilled and all knights that were left on live were come home again unto the Table Round, as the *Booke of the Sankgreall* maketh mention, then was there great joy in the court. And in especial king Arthur and queen Guenevere made great joy of the remnant that were come home, and passing glad was the king and the queen of sir Lancelot and of sir Bors, for they had been passing long away in the quest of the Sankgreall.

Then, as the book saith, sir Lancelot began to resort unto queen Guenevere again, and forgot the promise and the perfection that he made in the quest; for, as the book saith, had not sir Lancelot been in his privy thoughts and in his mind so set inwardly to the queen as he was in seeming outward to God, there had no knight passed him in the quest of the Sankgreall. But ever his thoughts privily were on the queen, and so they loved togethers more hotter than they did toforehand; and had many such privy draughts together that many in the court spoke of it, and in especial sir Agravain, sir Gawain's brother, for he was ever open-mouthed.

(But Lancelot is also the champion of many ladies, whom he helps 'for the pleasure of our Lord Jesus Christ.' The queen reproaches him for this and after a scene banishes him from her. He conceals himself in a hermitage near Windsor. The queen gives a banquet for twenty-four knights in which one of them attempts to kill Sir Gawain, who was known to love fruit, by inserting a poisoned apple. The apple is eaten by another knight, Sir Patrice, who dies. His cousin, Sir Mador de la Porte, accuses the queen of his murder. The queen now needs a champion, since Arthur must be the judge. ' "What aileth you" said the king, "that ye cannot keep Sir Lancelot upon your side?" ' Sir Bors takes up the challenge on behalf of the queen. He must fight the accuser; if he loses the queen will be judged guilty and burnt at the stake.

When Bors is about to begin the fight, 'then was he ware where came from

a wood there fast by a knight all armed, upon a white horse, with a strange
shield of strange arms, and he came driving all that his horse might run.'
The unknown knight champions the queen, defeats Sir Mador, and reveals
that he is Sir Lancelot. Sir Lancelot reconciles Sir Mador with the queen,
'and all was forgiven.')

2. *The Fair Maid of Astolat*

(Caxton XVIII, 8–20)

Thus it passed until our Lady day of the Assumption. Within a fifteen days of that feast the king let cry a great jousts and a tournament that should be at that day at Camelot, otherwise called Winchester, and the king let cry that he and the king of Scots would joust against all that would come against them. And when this cry was made, thither came many good knights, that is to say the king of North Wales, and king Anguish of Ireland, and the King with the Hundred Knights, and sir Galahalt the Haut Prince, and the king of Northumberland, and many other noble dukes and earls of other divers countries.

So king Arthur made him ready to depart to his jousts, and would have had the queen with him; but at that time she would not, she said, for she was sick and might not ride.

'That me repenteth,' said the king, 'for this seven year ye saw not such a noble fellowship togethers except the Whitsuntide when sir Galahad departed from the court.'

'Truly,' said the queen, 'ye must hold me excused. I may not be there, and that me repenteth.'*

And many deemed the queen would not be there because of sir Lancelot, for he would not ride with the king; for he said he was not whole of the play of sir Mador. Wherefore the king was heavy and passing wroth. And so he departed toward Winchester with his fellowship. And so by the way the king lodged at a town that was called Astolat, that is now in English called Guildford;* and there the king lay in the castle.

So when the king was departed the queen called sir Lancelot unto her and said thus:

'Sir, ye are greatly to blame thus to hold you behind my lord. What will your enemies and mine say and deem? "See how sir Lancelot holdeth him ever behind the king, and so the queen doth also, for that they would have their pleasure togethers." And thus will they say,' said the queen.

'Have ye no doubt, madam,' said sir Lancelot, 'I allow your wit. It is of late come sin ye were waxen so wise! And therefore, madam, at this time I will be ruled by your counsel, and this night I will take my rest, and tomorrow betime I will take my way toward Winchester. But wit you well,' said sir Lancelot unto the queen, 'at that jousts I will be against the king and against all his fellowship.'

'Sir, ye may there do as ye list,' said the queen, 'but by my counsel ye shall not be against your king and your fellowship, for there been full many hardy knights of your blood as ye wot wel enough—it needeth not to rehearse them.'*

'Madam,' said sir Lancelot, 'I pray you that ye be not displeased with me for I will take the adventure that God will send me.'*

And so upon the morn early sir Lancelot heard Mass and brake his fast, and so* took his leave of the queen and departed, and then he rode so much unto the time he came to Astolat. And there it happened him that in the evening-tide he came to an old baron's place that hight sir Bernard of Astolat. And as sir Lancelot entered into his lodging, king Arthur espied him as he did walk in a garden beside the castle. He knew him well enough.

'Well, sirs,' said king Arthur unto his knights that were by him beside the castle, 'I have now espied one knight,' he said, 'that will play his play at the jousts, to the which we be gone toward. I undertake he will do marvels'.*

'Who is that? We pray you tell us', said many knights that were there at that time.*

'Ye shall not wit for me!' said the king, 'as at this time'. And so the king smiled and went to his lodging.*

So when sir Lancelot was in his lodging and unarmed in his chamber, the old baron, sir Bernard, came to him and welcomed him in the best manner, but he knew not sir Lancelot.

'Fair sir,' said sir Lancelot till his host, 'I would pray you to lend me a shield that were not openly known, for mine is well known.'

'Sir,' said his host, 'ye shall have your desire, for meseemeth ye been one of the likeliest knights that ever I saw, and therefore, sir, I shall shew you friendship.' And he* said, 'Sir, wit you well I have two sons

that were but late made knights; and the eldest hight sir Tirry, and he
was hurt that same day he was made knight, and he may not ride.
And his shield ye shall have, for that is not known, I dare say, but here
and in no place else.' And his younger son hight sir Lavain. 'And if it
please you, he shall ride with you unto that jousts, for he is of his age
strong and wight. For much my heart giveth unto you, that ye should
be a noble knight, and therefore I pray you to tell me your name,'
said sir Bernard.

'As for that,' said sir Lancelot, 'ye must hold me excused as at this
time, and if God give me grace to speed well at the jousts I shall come
again and tell you my name. But I pray you in any wise let me have
your son sir Lavain with me, and that I may have his brother's shield.'

'Sir, all this shall be done,' said sir Bernard.

So this old baron had a daughter that was called that time the Fair
Maiden of Astolat. And ever she beheld sir Lancelot wonderfully, and,
as the book saith, she cast such a love unto sir Lancelot that she could
never withdraw her love, wherefore she died. And her name was
Elaine la Blanche. So thus as she came to and fro, she was so hot in
love that she besought sir Lancelot to wear upon him at the jousts a
token of hers.

'Damsel,' said sir Lancelot, 'and if I grant you that, ye may say that
I do more for your love than ever I did for lady or gentlewoman.'

Then he remembered himself that he would go to the jousts
disguised, and because he had never aforn borne no manner of token of
no damsel, he bethought him to bear a token of hers, that none of his
blood thereby might know him, and then he said:

'Fair maiden, I will grant you to wear a token of yours upon mine
helmet. And therefore what is it? Shew ye it me.'

'Sir,' she said, 'it is a red sleeve of mine, of scarlet, well embroidered
with great pearls.' And so she brought it him. So sir Lancelot received
it and said,

'Never did I erst so much for no damsel.'

Then sir Lancelot betook the fair maiden his shield in keeping, and
prayed her to keep it until time that he came again. And so that night
he had merry rest and great cheer, for this damsel Elaine was ever
about sir Lancelot all the while she might be suffered.

So upon a day, on the morn, king Arthur and all his knights departed,
for there the king had tarried three days to abide his noble knights.

And so when the king was ridden, sir Lancelot and sir Lavain made them ready to ride, and either of them had white shields, and the red sleeve sir Lancelot let carry with him. And so they took their leave at sir Bernard, the old baron, and at his daughter, the fair maiden, and then they rode so long till that they came to Camelot, that time called Winchester. And there was great press of kings, dukes, earls, and barons, and many noble knights, but sir Lancelot was lodged privily by the means of sir Lavain with a rich burgess, that no man in that town was ware what they were. And so they reposed them there till our Lady day of the Assumption that the great jousts should be.

So when trumpets blew unto the field and king Arthur was set on height upon a chafflet to behold who did best—but, as the French book saith, the king would not suffer sir Gawain to go from him, for never had sir Gawain the better and sir Lancelot were in the field, and many times was sir Gawain rebuked when sir Lancelot came in to any jousts disguised*—then some of the kings, as king Anguish of Ireland and the king of Scots, were that time turned to be upon the side of king Arthur. And then the other party was the king of North Wales, and the King with the Hundred Knights, and the king of Northumberland, and sir Galahalt the Haut Prince. But these three kings and this duke was passing weak to hold against Arthur's party, for with him were the noblest knights of the world. So then they withdrew them, either party from other, and every man made him ready in his best manner to do what he might.

Then sir Lancelot made him ready and put the red sleeve upon his helmet and fastened it fast. And so sir Lancelot and sir Lavain departed out of Winchester privily and rode until a little leaved wood behind the party that held against king Arthur party. And there they held them still till the parties smote togethers. And then came in the king of Scots and the king of Ireland on king Arthur's party, and against them came in the king of Northumberland and the King with the Hundred Knights. And there began a great medley, and there the king of Scots smote down the king of Northumberland, and the King with the Hundred Knights smote down king Anguish of Ireland. Then sir Palomides, that was one of Arthur's party, he encountered with sir Galahalt, and either of them smote down other, and either party holp their lords on horseback again. So there began a strong assail on both parties.

And then came in sir Brandiles, sir Sagramour le Desirous, sir Dodinas le Savage, sir Kay le Seneschal, sir Grifflet le Fitz de Dieu, sir Lucan de Butler, sir Bedivere, sir Agravain, sir Gaheris, sir Mordred, sir Meliot de Logres, sir Ozanna le Cure Hardy, sir Saphir, sir Epinogris, sir Galleron of Galway, all these fifteen knights, that were knights of the Round Table. So these with mo other came in together and beat aback the king of Northumberland and the king of North Wales.

When sir Lancelot saw this, as he hoved in the little leaved wood, then he said unto sir Lavain,

'See, yonder is a company of good knights, and they hold them togethers as boars that were chased with dogs.'

'That is truth,' said sir Lavain.

'Now,' said sir Lancelot, 'and ye will help a little, ye shall see the yonder fellowship that chaseth now these men on our side, that they shall go as fast backward as they went forward.'

'Sir, spare ye not for my part,' said sir Lavain, 'for I shall do what I may.'

Then sir Lancelot and sir Lavain came in at the thickest of the press, and there sir Lancelot smote down sir Brandiles, sir Sagramour, sir Dodinas, sir Kay, sir Grifflet, and all this he did with one spear. And sir Lavain smote down sir Lucan de Butler and sir Bedivere. And then sir Lancelot got another great spear, and there he smote down sir Agravain and sir Gaheris, sir Mordred, sir Meliot de Logres, and sir Lavain smote down sir Ozanna le Cure Hardy. And then sir Lancelot drew his sword, and there he smote on the right hand and on the left hand, and by great force he unhorsed sir Saphir, sir Epinogris, and sir Galleron. And then the knights of the Table Round withdrew them aback after they had gotten their horses as well as they might.

'A, mercy Jesu!' said sir Gawain, 'What knight is yonder that doth so marvellous deeds in that field?'

'I wot what he is,' said the king, 'but as at this time I will not name him.'

'Sir,' said sir Gawain, 'I would say it were sir Lancelot by his riding and his buffets that I see him deal, but ever meseemeth it should not be he, for that he beareth the red sleeve upon his helmet; for I wist him never bear token at no jousts of lady ne gentlewoman.'

'Let him be,' said king Arthur, 'for he will be better known and do more or ever he depart.'

Then the party that was against king Arthur were well comforted, and then they held them togethers, that befornhand were sore rebuked.

Then sir Bors, sir Ector de Maris and sir Lionel, they called unto them the knights of their blood, as sir Blamour de Ganis, sir Bleoberis, sir Aliduke, sir Galihud, sir Galihodin, sir Bellinger le Bewse. So these nine knights of sir Lancelot's kin thrust in mightily, for they were all noble knights, and they of great hate and despite that they had unto him thought to rebuke that noble knight* sir Lancelot, and sir Lavain, for they knew them not. And so they came hurling togethers and smote down many knights of North Wales and of Northumberland.

And when sir Lancelot saw them fare so, he got a great spear in his hand. And they encountered with him all at once, sir Bors, sir Ector, and sir Lionel. And they three smote him at once with their spears. And with force of themself they smote sir Lancelot's horse reverse to the earth. And by misfortune sir Bors smote sir Lancelot through the shield into the side, and the spear broke and the head left still in the side.

When sir Lavain saw his master lie on the ground he ran to the king of Scots and smote him to the earth, and by great force he took his horse and brought him to sir Lancelot, and maugre them all he made him to mount upon that horse. And then sir Lancelot got a spear in his hand, and there he smote sir Bors, horse and man, to the earth, and in the same wise he served sir Ector and sir Lionel. And sir Lavain smote down sir Blamor de Ganis. And then sir Lancelot drew his sword, for he felt himself so sore hurt that he went there to have had his death, and then he smote sir Bleoberis such a buffet on the helmet that he fell down to the earth in a swoon, and in the same wise he served sir Aliduke and sir Galihud. And sir Lavain smote down sir Bellinger that was son to Alexander le Orphelin.

And by this was done, was sir Bors horsed again and in came with sir Ector and sir Lionel, and all they three smote with their swords upon sir Lancelot's helmet. And when he felt their buffets, and with that his wound grieved him grievously, then he thought to do what he might while he could endure. And then he gave sir Bors such a buffet that he made him bow his head passing low, and therewithal he raced off his helm, and might have slain him; and so pulled him down. And in the same wise he served sir Ector and sir Lionel, for, as the book saith, he might have slain them, but when he saw their visages his heart might not serve him thereto, but left them there.

And then afterward he hurled into the thickest press of them all, and did there the marvelloust deeds of arms that ever man saw or heard speak of and ever sir Lavain the good knight* with him. And there sir Lancelot with his sword smote down and pulled down, as the French book saith, mo than thirty knights, and the most party were of the Table Round. And there sir Lavain did full well that day, for he smote down ten knights of the Table Round.

'Mercy Jesu,' said sir Gawain unto king Arthur, 'I marvel what knight that he is with the red sleeve.'

'Sir,' said king Arthur, 'he will be known or ever he depart.'

And then the king blew unto lodging, and the prize was given by heralds unto the knight with the white shield that bore the red sleeve. Then came the king of North Wales and the king of Northumberland, and the King with the Hundred Knights, and sir Galahalt the Haut Prince, and said unto sir Lancelot,

'Fair knight, God you bless, for much have ye done for us this day. And therefore we pray you that ye will come with us, that ye may receive the honour and the prize as ye have worshipfully deserved it.'

'Fair lords,' said sir Lancelot, 'wit you well, if I have deserved thank I have sore bought it, and that me repenteth it, for I am never like to escape with the life. Therefore, my fair lords, I pray you that ye will suffer me to depart where me liketh, for I am sore hurt. And I take no force of none honour, for I had liefer repose me than to be lord of all the world.' And therewithal he groaned piteously and rode a great gallop awayward from them until he came under a wood's eaves. And when he saw that he was from the field nigh a mile, that he was sure he might not be seen, then he said with an high voice and with a great groan,

'Ah, gentle knight, sir Lavain! Help me that this truncheon were out of my side, for it sticketh so sore that it nigh slayeth me!'

'Ah, mine own lord,' said sir Lavain, 'I would fain do that might please you, but I dread me sore, and I pull out the truncheon, that ye shall be in peril of death.'

'I charge you,' said sir Lancelot, 'as ye love me, draw it out!' And therewithal he descended from his horse, and right so did sir Lavain, and forwithal sir Lavain* drew the truncheon out of his side. And gave a great shriek and a grisly groan, that the blood burst out, nigh a pint at once, that at the last he sank down upon his arse and so swooned down, pale and deadly.

'Alas,' said sir Lavain, 'what shall I do?' And then he turned sir Lancelot into the wind, and so he lay there nigh half an hour as he had been dead. And so at the last sir Lancelot cast up his eyen and said,

'Ah, sir Lavain, help me that I were on my horse! For here is fast by, within this two mile, a gentle hermit that sometime was a full noble knight and a great lord of possessions. And for great goodness he hath taken him to wilful poverty and forsaken mighty lands, and his name is sir Baldwin of Brittany. And he is a full noble surgeon and a good leech. Now let see and help me up that I were there, for ever my heart giveth me that I shall never die of my cousin germain's hands.'

And then with great pain sir Lavain holp him upon his horse, and then they rode a great gallop togethers, and ever sir Lancelot bled, that it ran down to the earth. And so by fortune they came to an hermitage which was under a wood, and a great cliff on the other side, and a fair water running under it. And then sir Lavain beat on the gate with the butt of his spear and cried fast, 'Let in, for Jesu's sake!' And anon there came a fair child to them and asked them what they would.

'Fair son,' said sir Lavain, 'go and pray thy lord the hermit for God's sake to let in here a knight that is full sore wounded. And this day, tell thy lord, I saw him do more deeds of arms than ever I heard say that any man did.' So the child went in lightly. And then he brought the hermit which was a passing likely man. When sir Lavain saw him he prayed him for God's sake of succour.

'What knight is he?' said the hermit, 'Is he of the house of king Arthur or not?'

'I wot not,' said sir Lavain, 'what he is, nother what is his name, but well I wot I saw him do marvellously this day as of deeds of arms.'

'On whose party was he?' said the hermit.

'Sir,' said sir Lavain, 'he was this day against king Arthur, and there he won the prize of all the knights of the Round Table.'

'I have seen the day,' said the hermit, 'I would have loved him the worse because he was against my lord king Arthur, for sometime I was one of the fellowship. But now, I thank God, I am otherwise disposed. But where is he? Let me see him.'

Then sir Lavain brought the hermit to him. And when the hermit beheld him as he sat leaning upon his saddle-bow, ever bleeding spiteously, and ever the knight hermit thought that he should know him. But he could not bring him to knowledge because he was so pale for bleeding.

'What knight are ye?' said the hermit, 'and where were ye born?'

'My fair lord,' said sir Lancelot, 'I am a stranger, and a knight adventurous that laboureth throughout many realms for to win worship.'

Then the hermit avised him better, and saw by a wound on his cheek that he was sir Lancelot.

'Alas,' said the hermit, 'mine own lord! Why lain you your name from me? Perdeus, I ought to know you of right, for ye are the most noblest knight of the world. For well I know you for sir Lancelot.'

'Sir,' said he, 'sith ye know me, help me and ye may, for God's sake! For I would be out of this pain at once, other to death, other to life.'

'Have ye no doubt,' said the hermit, 'for ye shall live and fare right well.'

And so the hermit called to him two of his servants, and so they bore him into the hermitage, and lightly unarmed him, and laid him in his bed. And then anon the hermit staunched his blood and made him to drink good wine, that he was well revigoured and knew himself. For in those days it was not the guise as is nowadays, for there were none hermits in tho days but that they had been men of worship and of prowess, and tho hermits held great households and refreshed people that were in distress.

Now turn we unto king Arthur and leave we sir Lancelot in the hermitage. So when the kings were comen* togethers on both parties, and the great feast should be holden, king Arthur asked the king of North Wales and their fellowship where was that knight that bore the red sleeve. 'Let bring him before me, that he may have his laud and honour and the prize, as it is right.'

Then spoke sir Galahalt the Haut Prince and the King with the Hundred Knights, and said,

'We suppose that knight is mischieved so that he is never like to see you nother none of us all, and that is the greatest pity that ever we wist of any knight.'

'Alas,' said king Arthur, 'how may this be? Is he so sore hurt? But what is his name?' said king Arthur.

'Truly,' said they all, 'we know not his name, nother from whence he came, nother whither he would.'

'Alas,' said the king, 'this is the worst tidings that came to me this seven year! For I would not for all the lands I wield to know and wit it were so that that noble knight were slain.'

'Sir, know ye aught of him?' said they all.

'As for that,' said king Arthur, 'whether I know him other none, ye shall not know for me what man he is, but Almighty Jesu send me good tidings of him.'

And so said they all.

'By my head,' said sir Gawain, 'if it so be that the good knight be so sore hurt, it is great damage and pity to all this land, for he is one of the noblest knights that ever I saw in a field handle spear or sword. And if he may be found I shall find him, for I am sure he is not far from this country.'

'Sir, ye bear you well,' said king Arthur, 'and ye may find him, unless he be in such a plight that he may not wield himself.'

'Jesu defend!' said sir Gawain. 'But wit well I shall know what he is and I may find him.'

Right so sir Gawain took a squire with him upon hackneys and rode all about Camelot within six or seven mile, but so he came again and could hear no word of him. Then within two days king Arthur and all the fellowship returned unto London again. And so as they rode by the way it happened sir Gawain at Astolat to lodge with sir Bernard thereas was sir Lancelot lodged.

And so as sir Gawain was in his chamber to repose him, sir Bernard, the old baron, came in to him, and his daughter Elaine, to cheer him, and to ask him what tidings, and who did best at the tournament of Winchester.

'So God me help,' said sir Gawain, 'there were two knights that bore two white shields, but one of them bore a red sleeve upon his head, and certainly he was the best knight that ever I saw joust in field. For I dare say,' said sir Gawain, 'that one knight with the red sleeve smote down forty knights of the Round Table. And his fellow did right well and worshipfully.'

'Now blessed be God,' said this Fair Maiden of Astolat, 'that that

c

knight sped so well! For he is the man in the world that I first loved, and truly he shall be the last that ever I shall love.'

'Now, fair maiden,' said sir Gawain, 'is that good knight your love?'

'Certainly, sir,' she said, 'he is my love.'

'Then know ye his name?' said sir Gawain.

'Nay truly, sir,' said the damsel, 'I know not his name, nother from whence he came. But to say that I love him, I promise God and you I love him.'

'How had ye knowledge of him first?' said sir Gawain.

Then she told him, as ye have heard before; and how her father betook him her brother to do him service; and how her father lent him her brother's, sir Tirry's shield; 'and here with me he left his own shield.'

'For what cause did he so?' said sir Gawain.

'For this cause,' said the damsel, 'for his shield was full well known among many noble knights.'

'Ah, fair damsel,' said sir Gawain, 'please it you to let me have a sight of that shield?'

'Sir,' she said, 'it is in my chamber, covered with a case, and if ye will come with me ye shall see it.'

'Not so,' said sir Bernard to his daughter, 'but send ye for that shield.'

So when the shield was come sir Gawain took off the case, and when he beheld that shield, and knew it anon that it was sir Lancelot's shield and his own arms, 'Ah, Jesu mercy!' said sir Gawain, 'now is my heart more heavier than ever it was tofore.'

'Why?' said this maid Elaine.

'For I have a great cause,' said sir Gawain. 'Is that knight that oweth this shield your love?'

'Yea truly,' she said, 'my love is he. God would that I were his love!'

'So God me speed,' said sir Gawain, 'fair damsel, ye have right, for and he be your love, ye love the most honourablest knight of the world and the man of most worship.'

'So methought ever,' said the damsel, 'for never or that time no knight that ever I saw loved I never none erst.'

'God grant,' said sir Gawain, 'that either of you may rejoice other, but that is in a great aventure. But truly,' said sir Gawain unto the

damsel, 'ye may say ye have a fair grace, for why I have known that
noble knight this four-and-twenty year, and never or that day I nor
none other knight, I dare make good, saw never nother heard say that
ever he bore token or sign of no lady, gentlewoman, nor maiden at no
jousts nother tournament. And therefore, fair maiden, ye are much
beholden to him to give him thank. But I dread me,' said sir Gawain,
'that ye shall never see him in this world, and that is as great pity as
ever was of any earthly man.'

'Alas,' said she, 'how may this be? Is he slain?'

'I say not so,' said sir Gawain, 'but wit you well he is grievously
wounded by all manner of signs, and by men's* sight more likelier to
be dead than to be on live. And wit you well he is the noble knight
sir Lancelot, for by this shield I know him.'

'Alas,' said this Fair Maiden of Astolat, 'how may this be? And what
was his hurt?'

'Truly,' said sir Gawain, 'the man in the world that loved best him
hurt him. And I dare say,' said sir Gawain, 'and that knight that hurt
him knew the very certainty that he had hurt sir Lancelot, it were
the most sorrow that ever came to his heart.'

'Now, fair father,' said then Elaine, 'I require you give me leave to
ride and seek him, other else I wot well I shall go out of my mind.
For I shall never stint till that I find him and my brother, sir Lavain.'
'Do ye as it liketh you,' said her father, 'for sore me repents of the
hurt of that noble knight.' Right so the maid made her ready and
departed before sir Gawain making great dole.

Then on the morn sir Gawain came to king Arthur and told him all
how he had found sir Lancelot's shield in the keeping of the Fair Maiden
of Astolat. 'All that knew I aforehand,' said king Arthur, 'and that
caused me I would not suffer you to have ado at the great jousts; for
I espied him when he came until his lodging, full late in the evening,
into Astolat. But great marvel have I,' said king Arthur, 'that ever
he would bear any sign of any damsel, for or now I never heard say
nor knew that ever he bore any token of none earthly woman.'

'By my head, sir,' said sir Gawain, 'the Fair Maiden of Astolat
loveth him marvellously well. What it meaneth I cannot say. And
she is ridden after to seek him.'

So the king and all came to London, and there Gawain all openly
disclosed it to all the court that it was sir Lancelot that jousted best.

And when sir Bors heard that, wit you well he was an heavy man, and so were all his kinsmen. But when the queen wist that it was sir Lancelot that bore the red sleeve of the Fair Maiden of Astolat, she was nigh out of her mind for wrath, and then she sent for sir Bors de Ganis in all haste that might be. So when sir Bors was come before the queen she said,

'Ah, sir Bors! Have ye not heard say how falsely sir Lancelot hath betrayed me?'

'Alas, madam,' said sir Bors, 'I am afeared he hath betrayed himself and us all.'

'No force,' said the queen, 'though he be destroyed, for he is a false traitor knight.'

'Madam,' said sir Bors, 'I pray you say ye no more so, for wit you well I may not hear no such language of him.'

'Why so, sir Bors?' said she. 'Should I not call him traitor when he bore the red sleeve upon his head at Winchester at the great jousts?'

'Madam,' said sir Bors, 'that sleeve-bearing repents me, but I dare say he did bear it to none evil intent, but for this cause he bore the red sleeve, that none of his blood should know him. For or then we nother none of us all never knew that ever he bore token or sign of maiden, lady, nother gentlewoman.'

'Fie on him!' said the queen. 'Yet for all his pride and bobance, there ye proved yourself better man than he.'

'Nay, madam, say ye nevermore so, for he beat me and my fellows, and might have slain us and he had would.'

'Fie on him!' said the queen, 'for I heard sir Gawain say before my lord Arthur that it were marvel to tell the great love that is between the Fair Maiden of Astolat and him.'

'Madam,' said sir Bors, 'I may not warn sir Gawain to say what it pleaseth him, but I dare say, as for my lord sir Lancelot, that he loveth no lady, gentlewoman, nother maiden, but as he loveth all inlike much. And therefore, madam' said sir Bors, 'ye may say what ye will, but wit you well I will haste me to seek him and find him wheresomever he be, and God send me good tidings of him!'

And so leave we them there, and speak we of sir Lancelot that lay in great peril. And so as this fair maiden Elaine came to Winchester she sought there all about. And by fortune sir Lavain, her brother, was ridden to sport him to enchafe his horse, and anon as this maiden

Elaine saw him she knew him, and then she cried on-loud till him. And when he heard her he came to her, and anon with that she asked her brother, 'How doth my lord sir Lancelot?'

'Who told you, sister, that my lord's name was sir Lancelot?'

Then she told him how sir Gawain by his shield knew him. So they rode togethers till that they came to the hermitage, and anon she alight. So sir Lavain brought her in to sir Lancelot, and when she saw him lie so sick and pale in his bed she might not speak, but suddenly she fell down to the earth in a swough, and there she lay a great while. And when she was relieved she shrieked and said,

'My lord, sir Lancelot! Alas, why lie ye in this plight?' And then she swooned again. And then sir Lancelot prayed sir Lavain to take her up, 'and bring her hither to me.' And when she came to herself sir Lancelot lift her and said, 'Fair maiden, why fare ye thus? For ye put me to more pain. Wherefore make ye no such cheer, for and ye be come to comfort me, ye be right welcome. And of this little hurt that I have I shall be right hastily whole, by the grace of God. But I marvel,' said sir Lancelot, 'who told you my name.' And so this maiden told him all how sir Gawain was lodged with her father, 'and there by your shield he discovered your name.'

'Alas!' said sir Lancelot, 'that repenteth me that my name is known, for I am sure it will turn until anger.' And then sir Lancelot compassed in his mind that sir Gawain would tell queen Guenevere how he bore the red sleeve and for whom, that he wist well would turn unto great anger. So this maiden Elaine never went from sir Lancelot, but watched him day and night, and did such attendance to him that the French book saith there was never woman did nevermore kindlier for man than she.*

Then sir Lancelot prayed sir Lavain to make espies in Winchester for sir Bors if he came there, and told him by what tokens he should know him: by a wound in his forehead. 'For I am sure,' said sir Lancelot, 'that sir Bors will seek me, for he is the same good knight that hurt me.'

Now turn we unto sir Bors de Ganis, that came until Winchester to seek after his cousin sir Lancelot. And when he came to Winchester anon there were men that sir Lavain had made to lie in a watch for such a man and anon sir Lavain had warning. And then sir Lavain came to Winchester, and found sir Bors, and there he told him what he was, and with whom he was, and what was his name.* 'Now, fair knight,' said sir Bors, 'ye be welcome, and I require you that ye will bring me to my lord sir Lancelot.' 'Sir,' said sir Lavain, 'take your horse, and within this hour ye shall see him.'

So they departed and came to the hermitage. And when sir Bors saw sir Lancelot lie in his bed, dead pale and discoloured, anon sir Bors lost his countenance, and for kindness and pity he might not speak, but wept tenderly a great while. But when he might speak he said thus:

'Ah, my lord sir Lancelot, God you bless and send you hasty recovering! For full heavy am I of my misfortune and of mine unhappiness. For now I may call myself unhappy, and I dread me that God is greatly displeased with me, that he would suffer me to have such a shame for to hurt you that are all our leader and all our worship; and therefore I call myself unhappy. Alas, that ever such a caitiff knight as I am should have power by unhappiness to hurt the most noblest knight of the world! Where I so shamefully set upon you and overcharged you, and where ye might have slain me, ye saved me. And so did not I, for I and all our blood did to you their utterance. I marvel,' said sir Bors, 'that my heart or my blood would serve me. Wherefore, my lord sir Lancelot, I ask you mercy.'

'Fair cousin,' said sir Lancelot, 'ye be right welcome, and wit you well, overmuch ye say for the pleasure of me which pleaseth me nothing, for why I have the same ysought; for I would with pride have overcome you all. And there in my pride I was near slain, and that was in mine own default, for I might have given you warning of my being there, and then had I had no hurt. For it is an old-said saw, "there is hard battle thereas kin and friends doth battle either against other," for there may be no mercy but mortal war. Therefore, fair cousin,' said sir Lancelot, 'let this language overpass, and all shall be welcome that God sendeth. And let us leave off this matter and speak of some rejoicing, for this that is done may not be undone. And let us find a remedy how soon that I may be whole.'

Then sir Bors leaned upon his bed's side and told sir Lancelot how the queen was passing wroth with him, 'because ye wore the red sleeve at the great jousts.' And there sir Bors told him all how sir Gawain discovered it, 'by your shield that ye* left with the Fair Maiden of Astolat'. 'Then is the queen wroth?' said sir Lancelot.

'Therefore am I right heavy. But I deserved no wrath, for all that I did was because I would not be known.' 'Sir, right so excused I you,' said sir Bors 'but all was in vain, for she said more largelier to me than I to you say now. But, sir, is this she,' said sir Bors, 'that is so busy about you, that men call the Fair Maiden of Astolat?'

'Forsooth, she it is,' said sir Lancelot, 'that by no means I cannot put her from me.' 'Why should ye put her from you?' said sir Bors, 'for she is a passing fair damsel, and well beseen and well taught. And God would, fair cousin,' said sir Bors, 'that ye could love her. But as to that I may not nother dare not counsel you. But I see well,' said sir Bors, 'by her diligence about you that she loveth you entirely.' 'That me repents,' said sir Lancelot. 'Well,' said sir Bors, 'she is not the first that hath lost her pain upon you, and that is the more pity.' And so they talked of many mo things.

And so within three or four days sir Lancelot waxed big and light. Then sir Bors told sir Lancelot how there was sworn a great tournament betwixt king Arthur and the king of North Wales, that should be upon Allhallowmas day, besides Winchester.

'Is that truth?' said sir Lancelot. 'Then shall ye abide with me still a little while, until that I be whole, for I feel myself reasonably big and strong.' 'Blessed be God!' said sir Bors.

Then they were there nigh a month togethers, and ever this maiden Elaine did ever her diligence and labour both night and day unto sir Lancelot, that there was never child nother wife more meeker till father and husband than was this Fair Maiden of Astolat; wherefore sir Bors was greatly pleased with her.

So upon a day, by the assent of sir Lavain, sir Bors, and sir Lancelot, they made the hermit to seek in woods for divers herbs, and so sir Lancelot made fair Elaine to gather herbs for him to make him a bain. So in the meanwhile sir Lancelot made sir Lavain to arm him at all pieces, and there he thought to assay himself upon horseback with a spear, whether he might wield his armour and his spear for his hurt or not.

And so when he was upon his horse he stirred him freshly, and the horse was passing lusty and frick, because he was not laboured of a month before. And then sir Lancelot bade sir Lavain give him that great spear, and so sir Lancelot couched that spear in the rest. The courser leapt mightily when he felt the spurs; and he that was upon him, which was the noblest horseman of the world, strained him mightily and stably, and kept still the spear in the rest. And therewith sir Lancelot strained himself so straitly, with so great force, to get the courser forward that the bottom of his wound burst both within and without, and therewithal the blood came out so fiercely that he felt himself so feeble that he might not sit upon his horse. And then sir Lancelot cried unto sir Bors, 'Ah, sir Bors and sir Lavain, help! For I am come unto mine end!' And therewith he fell down on the one side to the earth like a dead corpse. And then sir Bors and sir Lavain came unto him with sorrow-making out of measure. And so by fortune this maiden, Elaine, heard their mourning, and then she came, and when she came, and when she found sir Lancelot there armed in that place she cried and wept as she had been wood. And then she kissed him and did what she might to awake him, and then she rebuked her brother and sir Bors, and called them false traitors, and said, 'Why would ye take him out of his bed? For and he die, I will appeal you of his death!'

And so with that came the hermit, sir Baldwin of Brittany, and when he found sir Lancelot in that plight he said but little, but wit you well he was wroth. But he said, 'Let us have him in,' and anon they bore him into the hermitage and unarmed him and laid him in his bed. And evermore his wound bled spiteously, but he stirred no limb of him. Then the knight hermit put a thing in his nose and a little deal of water in his mouth, and then sir Lancelot waked of his swough. And then the hermit staunched his bleeding, and when sir Lancelot might speak he asked why he put his life so in jeopardy.

'Sir,' said sir Lancelot, 'because I went I had be strong enough, and also sir Bors told me there should be at Allhallowmas a great jousts betwixt king Arthur and the king of North Wales. And therefore I thought to assay myself, whether I might be there or not.'

'Ah, sir Lancelot,' said the hermit, 'your heart and your courage will never be done until your last day! But ye shall do now by my counsel. Let sir Bors depart from you, and let him do at that tournament what he may. And, by the grace of God,' said the knight hermit, 'by that the tournament be done and he comen hither again, sir, ye shall be whole, so that ye will be governed by me.'

Then sir Bors made him ready to depart from him, and sir Lancelot said, 'Fair cousin, sir Bors, recommend me unto all tho ye ought recommend me unto, and I pray you enforce yourself at that jousts that ye may be best, for my love. And here shall I abide you, at the mercy of God, till your again-coming.'

And so sir Bors departed and came to the court of king Arthur, and told them in what place he left sir Lancelot. 'That me repents!' said the king. 'But sin he shall have his life, we all may thank God.'

And then sir Bors told the queen what jeopardy sir Lancelot was in when he would assay* his horse, 'and all that he did was for the love of you, because he would a been at this tournament.'

'Fie on him, recrayed knight!' said the queen. 'For wit you well I am right sorry and he shall have his life.'

'Madam, his life shall he have,' said sir Bors, 'and who that would otherwise, except you, madam, we that been of his blood would help to shorten their lives! But, madam,' said sir Bors, 'ye have been oftentimes displeased with my lord sir Lancelot, but at all times at the end ye found him a true knight.' And so he departed.

And then every knight of the Round Table that were there at* that time present made them ready to be at* that jousts at Allhallowmas, and thither drew many knights of divers countries. And as Allhallowmas drew near, thither came the king of North Wales, and the King with the Hundred Knights, and sir Galahalt the Haut Prince of Surluse. And thither came king Anguish of Ireland, and the king of Northumberland, and the king of Scots. So these three kings came to king Arthur's party.

And so that day sir Gawain did great deeds of arms and began first. And the heralds numbered that sir Gawain smote down twenty knights. Then sir Bors de Ganis came in the same time, and he was numbered he smote down twenty knights. And therefore the prize was given betwixt them both, for they began first and longest endured. Also sir Gareth, as the book saith, did that day great deeds of arms, for he smote down and pulled down thirty knights. But when he had done that deeds he tarried not, but so departed, and therefore he lost his prize. And sir Palomides did great deeds of arms that day, for he smote down twenty knights. But he departed suddenly, and men deemed that he and sir Gareth rode togethers to some manner adventures.

So when this tournament was done sir Bors departed, and rode till he came to sir Lancelot, his cousin. And then he found him walking

on his feet, and there either made great joy of other. And so Sir Bors*
told sir Lancelot of all the jousts, like as ye have heard.

'I marvel,' said sir Lancelot, 'that sir Gareth, when he had done
such deeds of arms, that he would not tarry.' 'Sir, thereof we marvelled
all,' said sir Bors, 'for but if it were you, other the noble knight sir
Tristram, other the good knight sir Lamorak de Wales, I saw never
knight bear so many knights and smite down in so little a while as
did sir Gareth. And anon as he was gone we all wist not where he
become.'

'By my head,' said sir Lancelot, 'he is a noble knight and a mighty
man and well breathed; and if he were well assayed,' said sir Lancelot,
'I would deem he were good enough for any knight that beareth the
life. And he is gentle, courteous and right bounteous, meek and mild,
and in him is no manner of mal engine, but plain, faithful and true.'

So then they made them ready to depart from the hermitage. And
so upon a morn they took their horses, and this Elaine la Blanche with
them. And when they came to Astolat there were they well lodged
and had great cheer of sir Bernard, the old baron, and of sir Tirry,
his son.

And so upon the morn, when sir Lancelot should depart, fair
Elaine brought her father with her, and sir Lavain, and sir Tirry, and
then thus she said: 'My lord, sir Lancelot, now I see ye will depart
from me. Now, fair knight and courteous knight,' said she, 'have
mercy upon me, and suffer me not to die for your love.'

'Why, what would ye that I did?' said sir Lancelot.

'Sir, I would have you to my husband,' said Elaine.

'Fair damsel, I thank you heartily,' said sir Lancelot, 'but truly,'
said he, 'I cast me never to be wedded man.'

'Then, fair knight,' said she, 'will ye be my paramour?'

'Jesu defend me!' said sir Lancelot, 'For then I rewarded your
father and your brother full evil for their great goodness.'

'Alas! then,' said she, 'I must die for your love.'

'Ye shall not do so,' said sir Lancelot, 'for wit you well, fair maiden,
I might have been married and I had would, but I never applied me
yet to be married. But because, fair damsel, that ye love me as ye say
ye do, I will for your good will and kindness shew to you some good-
ness. That is this, that wheresomever ye will beset your heart upon
some good knight that will wed you, I shall give you togethers a

thousand pounds yearly, to you and to your heirs. This much will I give you, fair maiden, for your kindness, and always while I live to be your own knight.'

'Sir, of all this,' said the maiden, 'I will none, for but if ye will wed me, other to be my paramour at the least, wit you well, sir Lancelot, my good days are done.'

'Fair damsel,' said sir Lancelot, 'of these two things ye must pardon me.'

Then she shrieked shrilly and fell down in a swough. And then women bore her into her chamber, and there she made overmuch sorrow. And then sir Lancelot would depart, and there he asked sir Lavain what he would do.

'Sir, what should I do,' said sir Lavain, 'but follow you, but if ye drive me from you or command me to go from you.'

Then came sir Bernard to sir Lancelot and said to him, 'I cannot see but that my daughter will die for your sake.'

'Sir, I may not do withal,' said sir Lancelot, 'for that me sore repenteth, for I report me to yourself that my proffer is fair. And me repenteth,' said sir Lancelot, 'that she loveth me as she doth, for I was never the causer of it. For I report me unto your son, I never early nother late proffered her bounty, nother fair behests. And as for me,' said sir Lancelot, 'I dare do all* that a knight should do, and say that she is a clean maiden for me, both for deed and will. For I am right heavy of her distress! For she is a full fair maiden, good and gentle and well ytaught.'

'Father,' said sir Lavain, 'I dare make good she is a clean maiden as for my lord sir Lancelot. But she doth as I do, for sithen I saw first my lord sir Lancelot I could never depart from him, neither naught I will, and I may follow him.'

Then sir Lancelot took his leave, and so they departed and came to Winchester. And when king Arthur wist that sir Lancelot was come whole and sound, the king made great joy of him, and so did sir Gawain and all the knights of the Round Table except sir Agravain and sir Mordred. Also queen Guenevere was wood wroth with sir Lancelot, and would by no means speak with him, but estranged herself from him. And sir Lancelot made all the means that he might for to speak with the queen, but it would not be.

Now speak we of the Fair Maiden of Astolat that made such sorrow day and night that she never slept, ate, nother drank, and ever she made her complaint unto sir Lancelot. So when she had thus endured a ten days, that she feebled so that she must needs pass out of this world, then she shrove her clean and received her Creator. And ever she complained still upon sir Lancelot. Then her ghostly father bade her leave such thoughts. Then she said:

'Why should I leave such thoughts? Am I not an earthly woman? And all the while the breath is in my body I may complain me, for my belief is that I do none offence, though I love an earthly man, unto God, for he formed me thereto, and all manner of good love cometh of God. And other than good love loved I never sir Lancelot du Lake. And I take God to record, I loved never none but him, nor never shall, of earthly creature. And a clean maiden I am for him and for all other. And sithen it is the sufferance of God that I shall die for so noble a knight, I beseech Thee, High Father of Heaven, have mercy upon me and my soul. And upon mine innumerable pains that I suffer may be allegiance of part of my sins, for sweet lord Jesu,' said the fair maiden, 'I take God to record I was never to Thee great offenser nother against Thy laws, but that I loved this noble knight, sir Lancelot, out of measure. And of myself, good Lord, I had no might to withstand the fervent love, wherefore I have my death!'

And then she called her father, sir Bernard, and her brother, sir Tirry, and heartily she prayed her father that her brother might write a letter like as she did endite, and so her father granted her. And when the letter was written, word by word like as she devised it, then she prayed her father that she might be watched until she were dead. 'And while my body is hot let this letter be put in my right hand, and my hand bound fast to the letter until that I be cold. And let me be put in a fair bed with all the richest clothes that I have about me, and so let my bed and all my richest clothes be led with me in a chariot unto the next place where the Thames is. And there let me be put within a barget, and but one man with me, such as ye trust, to steer me thither, and that my barget be covered with black samite over and over. And thus, father, I beseech you, let it be done.'

So her father grant her faithfully all thing should be done like as she had devised. Then her father and her brother made great dole for her. And when this was done, anon she died.

And when she was dead the corpse and the bed all was led the next way unto the Thames, and there a man and the corpse, and all thing as she had devised, was put in the Thames. And so the man stirred the barget unto Westminster, and there it rubbed and rolled to and fro a great while or any man espied it.

So by fortune king Arthur and queen Guenevere were talking togethers at a window, and so as they looked into the Thames they espied that black barget and had marvel what it meant. Then the king called sir Kay and shewed it him. 'Sir,' said sir Kay, 'wit you well, there is some new tidings.' 'Therefore go ye thither,' said the king to sir Kay, 'and take with you sir Brandiles and sir Agravain, and bring me ready word what is there.'

Then these three knights departed and came to the barget and went in. And there they found the fairest corpse lying in a rich bed that ever ye saw, and a poor man sitting in the barget's end, and no word would he speak. So these three knights returned unto the king again and told him what they found.

'That fair corpse will I see,' said the king. And so the king took the queen by the hand and went thither. Then the king made the barget to be hold fast, and then the king and the queen went in with certain knights with them. And there he saw the fairest woman lie in a rich bed, covered unto her middle with many rich clothes, and all was of cloth of gold. And she lay as she had smiled. Then the queen espied the letter in her right hand and told the king. Then the king took it and said, 'Now am I sure this letter will tell us what she was, and why she is come hither.'

So then the king and the queen went out of the barget, and so commanded a certain to wait upon the barget. And so when the king was come to his chamber he called many knights about him, and said that he would wit openly what was written within that letter. Then the king broke it, and made a clerk to read it, and this was the intent of the letter:

'Most noble knight, my lord sir Lancelot, now hath death made us two at debate for your love. And I was your lover, that men called the Fair Maiden of Astolat. Therefore unto all ladies I make my moan, yet for my soul ye pray and bury me at the least, and offer ye my masspenny. This is my last request. And a clean maiden I died, I take God to witness. And pray for my soul, sir Lancelot, as thou art peerless.'

This was all the substance in the letter. And when it was read the king, the queen and all the knights wept for pity of the doleful complaints. Then was sir Lancelot sent for, and when he was come king Arthur made the letter to be read to him. And when sir Lancelot heard it word by word, he said, 'My lord Arthur, wit you well I am right heavy of the death of this fair lady. And God knoweth I was never causer of her death by my willing, and that will I report me unto her own brother that here is, sir Lavain. I will not say nay,' said sir Lancelot, 'but that she was both fair and good, and much I was beholden unto her, but she loved me out of measure.'

'Sir,' said the queen, 'ye might have showed her some bounty and gentleness which might have preserved her life.'

'Madam,' said sir Lancelot, 'she would none other ways be answered but that she would be my wife, other else my paramour, and of these two I would not grant her. But I proffered her, for her good love that she showed me, a thousand pound yearly to her and to her heirs, and to wed any manner of knight that she could find best to love in her heart. For, madam,' said sir Lancelot, 'I love not to be constrained to love, for love must only arise of the heart self, and not by none constraint.'

'That is truth, sir,' said the king, 'and with many knights love is free in himself, and never will be bound; for where he is bound he looseth himself.'

Then said the king unto sir Lancelot, 'Sir, it will be your worship that ye oversee that she be interred worshipfully.'

'Sir,' said sir Lancelot, 'that shall be done as I can best devise.'

And so many knights yode thither to behold that fair dead maiden, and so upon the morn she was interred richly. And sir Lancelot offered her mass-penny; and all tho knights of the Table Round that were there at that time offered with sir Lancelot. And then the poor man went again with the barget.

Then the queen sent for sir Lancelot and prayed him of mercy, for why that she had been wroth with him causeless. 'This is not the first time,' said sir Lancelot, 'that ye have been displeased* with me causeless. But, madam, ever I must suffer you, but what sorrow that I endure, ye take no force.'

So this passed on all that winter, with all manner of hunting and hawking; and jousts and tourneys were many betwixt many great lords. And ever in all places sir Lavain got great worship, that he was nobly defamed among many knights of the Table Round.

Thus it passed on till Christmas, and then every day there was jousts made for a diamond: who that jousted best should have a diamond. But sir Lancelot would not joust but if it were a great jousts cried. But sir Lavain jousted there all the Christmas passingly well, and was best praised, for there were but few that did so well. Wherefore all manner of knights deemed that sir Lavain should be made knight of the Table Round at the next feast of Pentecost.

3. *The Great Tournament*
(Caxton XVIII, 21–4)

So at after Christmas king Arthur let call unto him many knights, and there they advised togethers to make a party and a great tournament and jousts. And the king of North Wales said to king Arthur he would have on his party king Anguish of Ireland and the King with the Hundred Knights and the king of Northumberland and sir Galahalt the Haut Prince. So these four kings and this mighty duke took party against king Arthur and the knights of the Round Table.

And the cry was made that the day of jousts should be besides Westminster, upon Candlemas day, whereof many knights were glad and made them ready to be at that jousts in the freshest manner.

Then queen Guenevere sent for sir Lancelot and said thus: 'I warn you that ye ride no more in no jousts nor tournaments but that your kinsmen may know you. And at this jousts that shall be ye shall have of me a sleeve of gold, and I pray you for my sake to force yourself there, that men may speak of* you worship. But I charge you, as ye will have my love, that ye warn your kinsmen that ye will bear that day the sleeve of gold upon your helmet.' 'Madam,' said sir Lancelot, 'it shall be done.' And other made great joy of other.

And when sir Lancelot saw his time he told sir Bors that he would depart, and no mo with him but sir Lavain, unto the good hermit that dwelled in the forest of Windsor, whose name was sir Brastias. And there he thought to repose him and to take all the rest that he might, because he would be fresh at that day of jousts. So sir Lancelot and sir Lavain departed, that no creature wist where he was become but the noble men of his blood. And when he was come to the hermitage, wit you well he had great cheer.

And so daily sir Lancelot used to go to a well fast* by the hermitage, and there he would lie down and see the well spring and burble, and some time he slept there. So at that time there was a lady that dwelled in that forest, and she was a great huntress, and daily she used to hunt. And ever she bore her bow with her, and no men went never with her, but always women, and they were all shooters and could well kill a deer at the stalk and at the tryst. And they daily bore bows, arrows, horns and wood-knives, and many good dogs they had, both for the string and for a bait.

So it happed the lady, the huntress, had abated her dog for the bow at a barren hind, and so this barren hind took the flight over heaths and woods. And ever this lady and part of her women coasted the hind, and checked it by the noise of the hound to have met with the hind at some water. And so it happened that that hind came to the same well thereas sir Lancelot was* sleeping and slumbering.

And so the hind, when she* came to the well, for heat she went to soil, and there she lay a great while. And the dog came after and umbecast about, for she had lost the very perfect fewte of the hind. Right so came that lady, the huntress, that knew by her dog that the hind was at the soil by that well, and thither she came straight and found the hind. And anon as she had spied her* she put a broad arrow in her bow, and shot at the hind, and so she overshot the hind, and so by misfortune the arrow smote sir Lancelot in the thick of the buttock over the barbs.

When sir Lancelot felt him so hurt, he whirled up woodly, and saw the lady that had smitten him. And when he knew she was a woman he said thus: 'Lady, or damsel, whatsomever ye be, in an evil time bore ye this bow. The devil made you a shooter!'

'Now mercy, fair sir!' said the lady, 'I am a gentlewoman that useth here in this forest hunting, and God knoweth I saw you not, but as here was a barren hind at the soil in this well. And I went I had done well, but my hand swerved.'

'Alas,' said sir Lancelot, 'ye have mischieved me!'

And so the lady departed. And sir Lancelot, as he might, pulled out the arrow and left the head still in his buttock, and so he went weakly unto the hermitage, evermore bleeding as he went. And when sir Lavain and the hermit espied that sir Lancelot was so sore hurt, wit you well they were passing heavy. But sir Lavain wist not how that he was hurt nother by whom. And then were they wroth out of measure. And so with great pain the hermit got out the arrow head out of sir Lancelot's buttock, and much of his blood he shed. And the wound was passing sore and unhappily smitten, for it was on such a place that he might not sit in no saddle.

'Ah, mercy Jesu!' said sir Lancelot, 'I may call myself the most unhappy man that liveth, for ever when I would have fainest worship there befalleth me ever some unhappy thing. Now, so Jesu me help,' said sir Lancelot, 'and if no man would but God, I shall be in the field on Candlemas day at the jousts, whatsomever fall of it.'

So all that might be gotten to heal sir Lancelot was had. So when the day was come sir Lancelot let devise that he was arrayed, and sir Lavain and he and their horses, as they had been Saracens. And so they departed and came nigh to the field.

So the king of North Wales he had a hundred knights with him, and the king of Northumberland brought with him an hundred good knights, and king Anguish of Ireland brought with him an hundred good knights ready to joust. And sir Galahalt the Haut Prince brought with him an hundred good knights, and the King with the Hundred Knights brought with him as many, and all these were proved good knights.

Then came in king Arthur's party, and in came with him the king of Scots, and an hundred knights with him, and king Uriens of Goore brought with him an hundred knights, and king Howell of Brittany he brought with him an hundred knights, and duke Chalence of Clarence brought with him an hundred knights. And king Arthur himself came into the field with two hundred knights, and the most party were knights of the Round Table that were all proved noble men. And there were old knights set on scaffolds for to judge with the queen who did best.

Then they blew unto the field. And there the king of North Wales encountered with the king of Scots, and there the king of Scots had a fall. And the king of Ireland smote down king Uriens, and the king of Northumberland smote down king Howell of Brittany, and sir Galahalt the Haut Prince smote down duke Chalence of Clarence. And then king Arthur was wood wroth, and ran to the King with the

Hundred Knights, and so king Arthur smote him down. And after with that same spear he smote down other three knights—and then his spear broke—and did passingly well.

So therewith came in sir Gawain and sir Gaheris, sir Agravain and sir Mordred, and there every of them smote down a knight and sir Gawain smote down four knights. And then there began a great medley, for then came in the knights of sir Lancelot's blood and sir Gareth and sir Palomides with them, and many knights of the Round Table. And they began to hold the four kings and the mighty duke so hard that were nigh discomfit. But this sir Galahalt the Haut Prince was a noble knight, and by his mighty prowess of arms he held the knights of the Round Table strait.

So all this doing saw sir Lancelot, and then he came into the field with sir Lavain with him, as it had been thunder. And then anon sir Bors and the knights of his blood espied sir Lancelot anon and said unto them all, 'I warn you, beware of him with the sleeve of gold upon his head, for he is himself my lord sir Lancelot.' And for great goodness sir Bors warned sir Gareth. 'Sir, I am well paid,' said sir Gareth, 'that I may know him.' 'But who is he,' said they all, 'that rideth with him in the same array?' 'Sir, that is the good and gentle knight sir Lavain,' said sir Bors.

So sir Lancelot encountered with sir Gawain, and there by force sir Lancelot smote down sir Gawain and his horse to the earth. And so he smote down sir Agravain and sir Gaheris, and also he smote down sir Mordred, and all this was with one spear. Then sir Lavain met with sir Palomides, and either met other so hard and so fiercely that both their horses fell to the earth. And then were they horsed again. And then met sir Lancelot with sir Palomides, and there sir Palomides had a fall.

And so sir Lancelot, or ever he stint, and as fast as he might get spears, he smote down thirty knights, and the most party were knights of the Round Table. And ever the knights of his blood withdrew them, and made them ado in other places where sir Lancelot came not.

And then king Arthur was wroth when he saw sir Lancelot do such deeds, and then the king called unto him sir Gawain, sir Gaheris, sir Agravain, sir Mordred, sir Kay, sir Grifflet, sir Lucan de Butler, sir Bedivere, sir Palomides and sir Saphir, his brother. And so the king with these nine knights made them ready to set upon sir Lancelot and upon sir Lavain.

And all this espied sir Bors and sir Gareth. 'Now I dread me sore,' said sir Bors, 'that my lord sir Lancelot will be hard matched.' 'Now by my head,' said sir Gareth, 'I will ride unto my lord sir Lancelot for to help him whatsomever me betide. For he is the same man that made me knight.' 'Sir, ye shall not do so,' said sir Bors, 'by my counsel, unless that ye were disguised.' 'Sir, ye shall see me soon disguised,' said sir Gareth.

And therwithal he had espied a Welsh knight where he was to repose him, for he was sore hurt before of sir Gawain. And unto him sir Gareth rode, and prayed him of his knighthood to lend him his shield for his. 'I will well,' said the Welsh knight.

And when sir Gareth had his shield—the book saith it was green with a maiden which seemed in it—then sir Gareth came driving unto sir Lancelot all that ever he might, and said,

'Sir knight, take keep to thyself, for yonder cometh king Arthur with nine noble knights with him, to put you to a rebuke. And so I am come to bear you fellowship for the old love ye have shewed unto me.' 'Grauntmercy,' said sir Lancelot. 'But, sir,' said sir Gareth, 'encounter ye with sir Gawain, and I shall encounter with sir Palomides, and let sir Lavain match with the noble king Arthur. And when we have delivered them let us three hold us sadly togethers.'

So then came in king Arthur with his nine knights with him, and sir Lancelot encountered with sir Gawain and gave him such a buffet that the arson of his saddle burst, and sir Gawain fell to the earth. Then sir Gareth encountered with sir Palomides, and he gave him such a buffet that both his horse and he dashed to the earth. Then encountered king Arthur with sir Lavain, and there either of them smote other to the earth, horse and all, that they lay both a great while.

Then sir Lancelot smote down sir Agravain and sir Gaheris and sir Mordred, and sir Gareth smote down sir Kay, sir Saphir and sir Grifflet. And then sir Lavain was horsed again, and he smote down sir Lucan de Butler and sir Bedivere, and then there began great throng of good knights. Then sir Lancelot hurled here and there, and raced and pulled off helms, that at that time there might none sit him a buffet with spear neither with sword. And sir Gareth did such deeds of arms that all men marvelled what knight he was with the green shield, for he smote down that day and pulled down mo than thirty knights. And, as the French book saith, sir Lancelot marvelled, when he beheld sir

Gareth do such deeds, what knight he might be. And sir Lavain smote and pulled down mo than twenty knights. And yet, for all this, sir Lancelot knew not sir Gareth; for and sir Tristram de Lyonesse other sir Lamorak de Wales had been on live, sir Lancelot would have deemed he had been one of them twain.

So ever as sir Lancelot, sir Gareth and sir Lavain fought on the tone side, sir Bors, sir Ector de Maris, sir Lionel, sir Bleoberis, sir Galihud, sir Galihodin and sir Pelleas and many mo other of king Banis blood fought upon another party and held the King with the Hundred Knights and the king of Northumberland right strait.

So this tournament and jousts dured long till it was near night, for the knights of the Round Table relieved ever unto king Arthur; for the king was wroth out of measure that he and his knights might not prevail that day. Then said sir Gawain to the king,

'Sir, I marvel where are all this day sir Bors de Ganis and his fellowship of sir Lancelot's blood, that of all this day they be not about you. And therefore I deem it is for some cause,' said sir Gawain.

'By my head,' said sir Kay, 'sir Bors is yonder all this day upon the right hand of this field, and there he and his blood doth more worshipfully than we do.'

'It may well be,' said sir Gawain, 'but I dread me ever of guile. For on pain of my life, that same knight with the red sleeve of gold is himself sir Lancelot, for I see well by his riding and by his great strokes. And the other knight in the same colours is the good young knight sir Lavain, and that knight with the green shield is my brother sir Gareth, and yet he hath disguised himself, for no man shall make him be against sir Lancelot, because he made him knight.'

'By my head,' said king Arthur, 'nephew, I believe you. And therefore now tell me what is your best counsel.'

'Sir,' said Gawain, 'my counsel is to blow unto lodging. For and he be sir Lancelot du Lake and my brother sir Gareth with him, with the help of that good young knight, sir Lavain, trust me truly, it will be no boot to strive with them but if we should fall ten or twelve upon one knight, and that were no worship, but shame.'

'Ye say truth,' said the king, 'it were shame for us, so many as we be, to set upon them any more. For wit you well,' said king Arthur, 'they be three good knights, and namely that knight with the sleeve of gold.'

And anon they blew unto lodging, but forthwithal king Arthur let send unto the four kings and to the mighty duke and prayed them that the knight with the sleeve of gold depart not from them 'but that the king may speak with him.' Then forthwithal king Arthur alight and unarmed him and took a little hackney and rode after sir Lancelot, for ever he had a spy upon him. And so he found him among the four kings and the duke, and there the king prayed them all unto supper, and they said they would with good will. And when they were unarmed king Arthur knew sir Lancelot, sir Gareth and sir Lavain. 'Ah, sir Lancelot,' said king Arthur, 'this day ye have heated me and my knights!'

And so they yode unto king Arthur's lodging all together, and there was a great feast and great revel. And the prize was given unto sir Lancelot, for by heralds they named him that he had smitten down fifty knights, and sir Gareth five-and-thirty knights, and sir Lavain four-and-twenty.

Then sir Lancelot told the king and the queen how the lady huntress shot him in the forest of Windsor in the buttock with a broad arrow, and how the wound was at that time six inches deep and inlike long.

Also king Arthur blamed sir Gareth because he left his fellowship and held with sir Lancelot. 'My lord,' said sir Gareth, 'he made me knight, and when I saw him so hard bestead, methought it was my worship to help him. For I saw him do so much deeds of arms, and so many noble knights against him, that when I understood that he was sir Lancelot du Lake I shamed to see so many good knights against him alone.'

'Now, truly,' said king Arthur unto sir Gareth, 'ye say well, and worshipfully have ye done, and to yourself great worship. And all the days of my life,' said king Arthur unto sir Gareth, 'wit you well I shall love you and trust you the more better. For ever it is,' said king Arthur, 'a worshipful knight's deed to help and succour another worshipful knight when he seeth him in danger. For ever a worshipful man will be loth to see a worshipful man shamed, and he that is of no worship and meddleth with cowardice never shall he shew gentleness nor no manner of goodness where he seeth a man in danger, for then will a coward never shew mercy. And always a good man will do ever to another man as he would be done to himself.'

So then there were made great feasts unto kings and dukes, and revel, game and play, and all manner of noblesse was used. And he that was courteous, true and faithful to his friend was that time cherished.

4. The Knight of the Cart
(Caxton XVIII, 25; XIX, 1–9)

And thus it passed on from Candlemas until after Easter, that the month of May was come, when every lusty heart beginneth to blossom and to burgeon. For, like as trees and herbs burgeoneth and flourisheth in May, in like wise every lusty heart that is any manner of lover springeth, burgeoneth, buddeth, and flourisheth in lusty deeds. For it giveth unto all lovers courage, that lusty month of May, in something to constrain him to some manner of thing more than in any other month, for divers causes: for then all herbs and trees reneweth a man and woman, and in like wise lovers calleth to their mind old gentleness and old service, and many kind deeds that was forgotten by negligence.

For, like as winter rasure doth alway erase and deface green summer, so fareth it by unstable love in man and woman, for in many persons there is no stability: for we may see all day, for a little blast of winter's rasure, anon we shall deface and lay apart true love, for little or nought, that cost much thing. This is no wisdom nother no stability, but it is feebleness of nature and great disworship, whosom-ever useth this.

Therefore, like as May month flowereth and flourisheth in every man's garden, so in like wise let every man of worship flourish his heart in this world: first unto God, and next unto the joy of them that he promised his faith unto; for there was never worshipful man nor worshipful woman but they loved one better than another; and worship in arms may never be foiled. But first reserve the honour to God, and secondly thy quarrel must come of thy lady. And such love I call virtuous love.

But nowadays men cannot love sevennight but they must have all their desires. That love may not endure by reason, for where they beeth soon accorded and hasty, heat soon cooleth. And right so fareth the love nowadays, soon hot soon cold. This is no stability. But the old love was not so. For men and women could love togethers seven years, and no licorous lusts was betwixt them, and then was love, truth and faithfulness. And lo* in like wise was used such love in king Arthur's days.

Wherefore I liken love nowadays unto summer and winter: for, like as the tone is cold and the other is hot, so fareth love nowadays. And therefore all ye that be lovers, call unto your remembrance the month of May, like as did queen Guenevere, for whom I make here a little mention, that while she lived she was a true lover, and therefore she had a good end.

So it befell in the month of May, queen Guenevere called unto her ten knights of the Table Round, and she gave them warning that early upon the morn she would ride on maying into woods and fields besides Westminster: 'And I warn you that there be none of you but he be well horsed, and that ye all be clothed all in green, other in silk other in cloth. And I shall bring with me ten ladies, and every knight shall have a lady by him. And every knight shall have a squire and two yeomen, and I will that all be well horsed.'

So they made them ready in the freshest manner, and these were the names of the knights: sir Kay le Seneschal, sir Agravain, sir Brandiles, sir Sagramour le Desirous, sir Dodinas le Savage, sir Ozanna le Cure Hardy, sir Ladinas of the Forest Savage, sir Persant of Ind, sir Ironside that was called the Knight of the Red Lands, and sir Pelleas the Lover. And these ten knights made them ready in the freshest manner to ride with the queen.

And so upon the morn or it were day, in a May morning, they took their horses with the queen and rode on maying in woods and meadows as it pleased them, in great joy and delights. For the queen had cast to have been again with king Arthur at the furthest by ten of the clock, and so was that time her purpose.

Then there was a knight which hight sir Meliagaunt, and he was son unto king Bagdemagus, and this knight had that time a castle of the gift of king Arthur within seven mile of Westminster. And this knight sir Meliagaunt loved passingly well queen Guenevere, and so had he done long and many years. And the book saith he had lain in await for to steal away the queen, but evermore he forbore for because of sir Lancelot; for in no wise he would meddle with the queen and sir Lancelot were in her company other else and he were nearhand.

And that time was such a custom that the queen rode never without a great fellowship of men of arms about her. And they were many good knights, and the most party were young men that would have worship, and they were called the Queen's Knights. And never in no battle, tournament nother jousts they bore none of them no manner of knowledging of their own arms, but plain white shields, and thereby they were called the Queen's Knights. And when it happed any of them to be of great worship by his noble deeds, then at the next feast of Pentecost, if there were any slain or dead (as there was none year that there failed but there were some dead), then was there chosen in his stead that was dead the most men of worship that were called the Queen's Knights. And thus they came up first or they were renowned men of worship, both sir Lancelot and all the remnant of them.

But this knight sir Meliagaunt had espied the queen well, and her purpose, and how sir Lancelot was not with her, and how she had no men of arms with her but the ten noble knights all arrayed in green for maying. Then he purveyed him a twenty men of arms and an hundred archers for to distress the queen and her knights; for he thought that time was best season to take the queen.

So as the queen was out on maying with all her knights which were bedashed with herbs, mosses and flowers in the best manner and* freshest, right so there came out of a wood sir Meliagaunt with an eight score men, well* harnessed as they should fight in a battle of arrest, and bade the queen and her knights abide, for maugre their heads they should abide.

'Traitor knight,' said queen Guenevere, 'what cast thou to do? Wilt thou shame thyself? Bethink thee how thou art a king's son and a knight of the Table Round, and thou thus to be about to dishonour the noble king that made thee knight! Thou shamest all knighthood and thyself and me. And I let thee wit thou shalt never shame me, for I had liefer cut mine own throat in twain rather than thou should dishonour me!'

'As for all this language,' said sir Meliagaunt, 'be as it be may. For wit you well, madam, I have loved you many a year, and never or now could I get you at such avail. And therefore I will take you as I find you.'

Then spoke all the ten noble knights at once and said, 'Sir Meliagaunt, wit thou well thou are about to jeopardy thy worship to dishonour, and also ye cast to jeopardy our persons. Howbeit we be unarmed and ye have us at a great advantage—for it seemeth by you that ye have laid watch upon us—but rather than ye should put the queen to a shame and us all, we had as lief to depart from our lives, for and we otherwise did we were shamed for ever.' Then said sir Meliagaunt, 'Dress you as well as ye can, and keep the queen!'

Then the ten knights of the Round Table drew their swords, and these other let run at them with their spears, and the ten knights manly abode them, and smote away their spears, that no spear did them no harm. Then they lashed togethers with swords, and anon sir Kay, sir Sagramour, sir Agravain, sir Dodinas, sir Ladinas and sir Ozanna were smitten to the earth with grimly wounds. Then sir Brandiles and sir Persant, sir Ironside and sir Pelleas fought long, and they were sore wounded, for these ten knights, or ever they were laid to the ground, slew forty men of the boldest and the best of them.

So when the queen saw her knights thus dolefully wounded and needs must be slain at the last, then for very pity and sorrow she cried and said,

'Sir Meliagaunt, slay not my noble knights! And I will go with thee upon this covenant: that thou save them and suffer them no more to be hurt, with this that they be led with me wheresomever thou leadest me. For I will rather slay myself than I will go with thee, unless that these noble knights may be in my presence.'

'Madam,' said sir Meliagaunt, 'for your sake they shall be led with you into mine own castle, with that ye will be ruled and ride with me.'

Then the queen prayed the four knights to leave their fighting, and she and they would not depart. 'Madam,' said sir Pelleas, 'we will do as ye do, for as for me, I take no force of my life nor death.' For, as the French book saith, sir Pelleas gave such buffets there that none armour might hold him.

Then by the queen's commandment they left battle and dressed the wounded knights on horseback, some sitting and some overthwart their horses, that it was pity to behold. And then sir Meliagaunt charged the queen and all her knights that none of her fellowship should depart from her, for full sore he dread sir Lancelot du Lake, lest he should have any knowledging. And all this espied the queen, and privily she called unto her a child of her chamber which was swiftly horsed of a great advantage.

'Now go thou,' said she, 'when thou seest thy time, and bear this ring unto sir Lancelot du Lake, and pray him as he loveth me that he will see me and rescue me, if ever he will have joy of me. And spare not thy horse,' said the queen, 'nother for water nother for land.'

So this child espied his time, and lightly he took his horse with spurs and departed as fast as he might. And when sir Meliagaunt saw him so flee, he understood that it was by the queen's commandment for to warn sir Lancelot. Then they that were best horsed chased him and shot at him, but from them all the child went deliverly.

And then sir Meliagaunt said unto the queen, 'Madam, ye are about to betray me, but I shall ordain for sir Lancelot that he shall not come lightly at you.'

And then he rode with her and all the fellowship in all the haste that they might. And so by the way sir Meliagaunt laid in bushment of the best archers that he might get in his country to the number of a thirty to await upon sir Lancelot, charging them that if they saw such a manner of* knight come by the way upon a white horse, 'that in any wise ye slay his horse, but in no manner have ye ado with him bodily, for he is over hardy to be overcome.' So this was done, and they were come to his castle. But in no wise the queen would never let none of the ten knights and her ladies out of her sight, but always they were in her presence. For the book saith sir Meliagaunt durst make no masteries for dread of sir Lancelot, insomuch he deemed that he had warning.

So when the child was departed from the fellowship of sir Meliagaunt, within a while he came to Westminster, and anon he found sir Lancelot. And when he had told his message and delivered him the queen's ring, 'Alas,' said sir Lancelot, 'now am I shamed for ever, unless that I may rescue that noble lady from dishonour!' Then eagerly he asked his arms.

And ever the child told sir Lancelot how the ten knights fought marvellously, and how sir Pelleas, sir Ironside, sir Brandiles and sir Persaunt of Ind fought strongly, but namely sir Pelleas—there might none harness hold him. And how they all fought till at the last* they were laid to the earth, and then* the queen made appointment for to save their lives and to go with sir Meliagaunt. 'Alas!' said sir Lancelot, 'that most noble lady, that she should be so destroyed! I had liefer,' said sir Lancelot, 'than all France that I had been there well armed.'

So when sir Lancelot was armed and upon his horse, he prayed the child of the queen's chamber to warn sir Lavain how suddenly he was departed and for what cause. 'And pray him as he loveth me, that he will hie him after me, and that he stint not until he come to the castle where sir Meliagaunt abideth, for there,' said sir Lancelot, 'he shall hear of me and I be a man living, and then shall I rescue the queen and the ten knights the which he traitorly hath taken, and that shall I prove upon his head, and all of them that hold with him.'

And then sir Lancelot rode as fast as he might, and the book saith he took the water at Westminster Bridge and made his horse swim over the Thames unto Lambeth. And so within a while he came to the same place thereas the ten noble knights fought with sir Meliagaunt. And then sir Lancelot followed the track until that he came to a wood, and there was a strait way. And there the thirty archers bade sir Lancelot turn again and follow no longer that track.

'What commandment have ye,' said sir Lancelot, 'to cause me, that am a knight of the Round Table, to leave my right way?'

'This ways shalt thou leave, other else thou shalt go it on thy foot, for wit thou well thy horse shall be slain.'

'That is little mastery,' said sir Lancelot, 'to slay mine horse! But as for myself, when my horse is slain I give right nought of you, not and ye were five hundred mo!'

So then they shot sir Lancelot's horse and smote him with many arrows, and then sir Lancelot avoided his horse and went on foot. But there were so many ditches and hedges betwixt them and him that he might not meddle with none of them.

'Alas, for shame!' said sir Lancelot, 'that ever one knight should betray another knight! But it is an old-said saw: "A good man is never in danger but when he is in the danger of a coward." '

Then sir Lancelot walked on a while, and was sore accumbered of his armour, his shield, and his spear and all that longed unto him.* Wit you well he was full sore annoyed! And full loth he was for to leave anything that longed unto him, for he dread sore the treason of sir Meliagaunt.

Then by fortune there came by him a chariot that came thither to fetch wood. 'Say me, carter,' said sir Lancelot, 'what shall I give thee to suffer me to leap into thy chariot, and that thou wilt bring me unto a castle within this two mile?'

'Thou shalt not enter into this chariot,' said the carter, 'for I am sent for to fetch wood.'

'Unto whom?' said sir Lancelot.

'Unto my lord, sir Meliagaunt,' said the carter.

'And with him would I speak,' said sir Lancelot.

'Thou shalt not go with me!' said the carter.

When sir Lancelot lep to him and gave him backward with his gauntlet a rearmaine, that he fell to the earth stark dead, then the tother carter, his fellow, was afeared, and went to have gone the same way. And then he cried,* 'Fair lord, save my life, and I shall bring you where ye will.'

'Then I charge thee,' said sir Lancelot, 'that thou drive me and this chariot unto sir Meliagaunt gate.' 'Then leap ye up into the chariot,' said the carter, 'and ye shall be there anon.' So the carter drove on a great gallop, and sir Lancelot's horse followed the chariot, with mo than forty arrows in him.

And more than an hour and an half queen Guenevere was awaiting in a bay-window. Then one of her ladies espied an armed knight standing in a chariot. 'Ah! see, madam,' said the lady, 'where rides in a chariot a goodly armed knight, and we suppose he rideth unto hanging.'

'Where?' said the queen.

Then she espied by his shield that he was there himself, sir Lancelot du Lake.* And then was she ware where came his horse after the chariot, and ever he trod his guts and his paunch under his feet.

'Alas!' said the queen, 'now I may prove and see that well is that creature that hath a trusty friend. Ha! a most noble knight',* said queen Guenevere, 'I see well that ye were hard bestead when ye ride in a chariot.' And then she rebuked that lady that likened sir Lancelot to ride in a chariot to hanging. 'Forsooth, it was foul-mouthed,' said the queen, 'and evil likened, so for to liken the most noble knight of the world unto such a shameful death. Ah! Jesu defend him and keep him,' said the queen, 'from all mischievous end!'

So by this was sir Lancelot comen to the gates of that castle, and there he descended down and cried, that all the castle might ring:

'Where art thou, thou false traitor sir Meliagaunt, and knight of the Table Round? Come forth, thou traitor knight, thou and all thy fellowship with thee, for here I am, sir Lancelot du Lake, that shall fight with you all!'

And therewithal he bore the gate wide open upon the porter and smote him under the ear with his gauntlet, that his neck burst in two pieces.

When sir Meliagaunt heard that sir Lancelot was comen, he ran unto the queen and fell upon his knee and said, 'Mercy, madam, for now I put me wholly in your good grace.'

'What ails you now?' said queen Guenevere, 'Pardé, I might well wit that some good knight would revenge me, though my lord king Arthur knew not of this your work.'

'Ah! madam,' said sir Meliagaunt, 'all this that is amiss on my party shall be amended right as yourself will devise, and wholly I put me in your grace.' 'What would ye that I did?' said the queen. 'Madam, I would no more,' said sir Meligaunt, 'but that ye would take all in your own hands, and that ye will rule my lord sir Lancelot. And such cheer as may be made him in this poor castle ye and he shall have until to-morn, and then may ye and all they return again unto Westminster. And my body and all that I have I shall put in your rule.' 'Ye say well,' said the queen, 'and better is peace than evermore war, and the less noise the more is my worship.'

Then the queen and her ladies went down unto sir Lancelot that stood wroth out of measure in the inner court to abide battle, and ever he said, 'Thou traitor knight, come forth!' Then the queen came unto him and said,

'Sir Lancelot, why be ye so amoved?'

'Ah! madam,' said sir Lancelot, 'why ask ye me that question? For meseemeth ye ought to be more wrother than I am, for ye have the hurt and the dishonour. For wit you well, madam, my hurt is but little in regard for the slaying of a mare's son, but the despite grieveth me much more than all my hurt.'

'Truly,' said the queen, 'ye say truth. But heartily I thank you,' said the queen. 'But ye must come in with me peaceably, for all thing is put in mine hand, and all that is amiss shall be amended, for the knight full sore repents him of this misadventure that is befallen him.'

'Madam,' said sir Lancelot, 'sith it is so that ye be accorded with him, as for me I may not againsay it, howbeit sir Meliagaunt hath done full shamefully to me and cowardly. And, madam,' said sir Lancelot, 'and I had wist that ye would have been so lightly accorded with him, I would not a made such haste unto you.'

'Why say ye so?' said the queen. 'Do ye forethink yourself of your good deeds? Wit you well,' said the queen, 'I accorded never with him for no favour nor love that I had unto him, but of every shameful noise, of wisdom, to lay adown.'

'Madam,' said sir Lancelot, 'ye understand full well I was never willing nor glad of shameful slander nor noise. And there is nother king, queen, ne knight that beareth the life, except my lord king Arthur and you, madam, that should let me but I should make sir Meliagaunt heart full cold or ever I departed from hence.'

'That wot I well,' said the queen, 'but what will ye more? Ye shall have all thing ruled as ye list to have it.'

'Madam,' said sir Lancelot, 'so ye be pleased I care not.* As for my part ye shall soon please me.'

Right so the queen took sir Lancelot by the bare hand, for he had put off his gauntlet. And so she went with him till her chamber, and then she commanded him to be unarmed. And then sir Lancelot asked the queen where were her ten knights that were wounded with her. Then she shewed them unto sir Lancelot,* and there they made great joy of the coming of him, and sir Lancelot made great dole of their hurts and bewailed them greatly.* And there sir Lancelot told them how cowardly and traitorly Meliagaunt* set archers to slay his horse, and how he was fain to put himself in a chariot. And thus they complained every to other, and full fain they would have been revenged, but they peaced themself* because of the queen.

Then, as the French book saith, sir Lancelot was called many days after 'le Chevalier de Chariot' and so he did many deeds and great adventures. And so we leave off here of le chevalier de chariot, and turn we to this tale.

So sir Lancelot had great cheer with the queen. And then he made a promise with the queen that the same night he should come to a window outward toward a garden, and that window was barred with iron. And there sir Lancelot promised to meet her when all folks were on sleep.

So then came sir Lavain driving to the gates, crying* 'Where is my lord sir Lancelot?' And anon he was sent for, and when sir Lavain saw sir Lancelot, he said, 'Ah! my lord! I found how ye were hard bestead, for I have found your horse that is slain with arrows.' 'As for that,' said sir Lancelot, 'I pray you, sir Lavain, speak ye of other matters and let this pass, and we shall* right it another time and we may.'

Then the knights that were hurt were searched, and soft salves were laid to their wounds, and so it passed on till supper-time. And all the cheer that might be made them there was done unto the queen and all her knights. And when season was they went unto their chambers, but in no wise the queen would not suffer her wounded knights to be from her, but that they were laid inwith draughts by her chamber, upon beds and pallets, that she might herself see unto them that they wanted nothing.

So when sir Lancelot was in his chamber which was assigned unto him, he called unto him sir Lavain and told him that night he must speak with his lady, queen Guenevere. 'Sir,' said sir Lavain, 'let me go with you, and it please you, for I dread me sore of the treason of sir Meliagaunt.' 'Nay,' said sir Lancelot, 'I thank you, but I will have nobody with me.'

Then sir Lancelot took his sword in his hand and privily went to the place where he had spied a ladder toforehand, and that he took under his arm, and bore it through the garden and set it up to the window. And anon the queen was there ready to meet him.

And then they made either to other* their complaints of many divers things, and then sir Lancelot wished that he might have comen in to her.

'Wit you well,' said the queen, 'I would as fain as ye that ye might come in to me.'

'Would ye so, madam,' said sir Lancelot, 'with your heart that I were with you?'

'Yea, truly,' said the queen.

'Then shall I prove my might,' said sir Lancelot, 'for your love.'

And then he set his hands upon the bars of iron and pulled at them with such a might that he burst them clean out of the stone walls. And therewithal one of the bars of iron cut the brawn of his hands throughout to the bone. And then he lep into the chamber to the queen.

'Make ye no noise,' said the queen, 'for my wounded knights lie here fast by me.'

So, to pass upon this tale, sir Lancelot went to bed with the queen and took no force of his hurt hand, but took his pleasance and his liking until it was the dawning of the day; for wit you well he slept not, but watched. And when he saw his time, that he might tarry no longer, he took his leave and departed at the window, and put it together as well as he might again, and so departed until his own chamber. And there he told sir Lavain how that he was hurt. Then sir Lavain dressed his hand and staunched it and put upon it a glove, that it should not be espied. And so they lay long a-bed in the morning till it was nine of the clock.

Then sir Meliagaunt went to the queen's chamber and found her ladies there ready clothed. 'Ah! Jesu mercy!' said sir Meliagaunt, 'what ails you, madam, that ye sleep this long?'

And therewithal he opened the curtain for to behold her. And then was he ware where she lay, and all the head-sheet, pillow, and over-sheet was all bebled of the blood of sir Lancelot and of his hurt hand. When sir Meliagaunt espied that blood, then he deemed in her that she was false to the king and that some of the wounded knights had lain by her all that night.

'Ah ha, madam!' said sir Meliagaunt, 'now I have found you a false traitress unto my lord Arthur, for now I prove well it was not for nought that ye laid these wounded knights within the bounds of your chamber. Therefore I will* call you of treason afore my lord king Arthur. And now I have proved you, madam, with a shameful deed; and that they been all false, or some of them, I will make it good, for a wounded knight this night hath lain by you.'

'That is false,' said the queen, 'that I will report me unto them.'

But when the ten knights heard sir Meliagaunt's words, then they spoke all at once and said, 'Sir Meliagaunt, thou falsely beliest my lady, the queen, and that we will make good upon thee, any of us. Now choose which thou list of us, when we are whole of the wounds thou gavest us.'

'Ye shall not! Away with your proud language! For here ye may all see that a wounded knight this night hath lain by the queen.'

Then they all looked and were sore ashamed when they saw that blood. And wit you well sir Meliagaunt was passing glad that he had the queen at such advantage, for he deemed by that to hide his own treason. And so in this rumour came in sir Lancelot and found them at a great affray.

'What array is this?' said sir Lancelot. Then sir Meliagaunt told them what he had found, and so he shewed him the queen's bed.

'Now truly,' said sir Lancelot, 'ye did not your part nor knightly, to touch a queen's bed while it was drawn and she lying therein. And I daresay,' said sir Lancelot, 'my lord king Arthur himself would not have displayed her curtains, and she being within her bed, unless that it had pleased him to have lain him down by her. And therefore, sir Meliagaunt, ye have done unworshipfully and shamefully to yourself.'

'Sir, I wot not what ye mean,' said sir Meliagaunt, 'but well I am sure there hath one of her hurt knights lain with her this night. And that will I prove with mine hands, that she is a traitress unto my lord king Arthur.'

'Beware what ye do,' said sir Lancelot, 'for and ye say so and will prove it, it will be taken at your hands.'

'My lord sir Lancelot,' said sir Meliagaunt, 'I rede you beware what ye do; for though ye are never so good a knight, as I wot well ye are renowned the best knight of the world, yet should ye be advised to do battle in a wrong quarrel, for God will have a stroke in every battle.'

'As for that,' said sir Lancelot, 'God is to be dread! But as to that I say nay plainly, that this night there lay none of these ten knights wounded with my lady queen Guenevere, and that will I prove with mine hands that ye say untruly in that. Now, what say ye?' said sir Lancelot.

'This I say,' said sir Meliagaunt, 'here is my glove that she is a traitress unto my lord king Arthur, and that this night one of the wounded knights lay with her.'

'Well, sir, and I receive your glove,' said sir Lancelot. And anon they were sealed with their signets, and delivered unto the ten knights. 'At what day shall we do battle togethers?' said sir Lancelot.

'This day eight days,' said sir Meliagaunt, 'in the field besides Westminster.' 'I am agreed,' said sir Lancelot. 'But now,' said sir Meliagaunt, 'sithen it is so that we must needs fight togethers, I pray you as ye beeth a noble knight, await me with no treason nother no villainy the meanwhile, nother none for you'. 'So God me help,' said sir Lancelot, 'ye shall right well wit that I was never of no such conditions. For I report me to all knights that ever have known me, I fared never with no treason, nother I loved never the fellowship of him that fared with treason.' 'Then let us go into dinner,' said sir Meliagaunt,

D

'and after dinner the queen and ye may ride all unto Westminster.'
'I will well,' said sir Lancelot.

Then sir Meliagaunt said unto sir Lancelot, 'Sir, pleaseth you to
see the* estres of this castle?' 'With a good will,' said sir Lancelot.

And then they went together from chamber to chamber, for sir
Lancelot dread no perils: for ever a man of worship and of prowess
dreads but little of perils, for they ween that every man be as they
been. But ever he that fareth with treason putteth often a true man in
great danger. And so it befell upon sir Lancelot that no peril dread:
as he went with sir Meliagaunt he trod on a trap, and the board rolled,
and there sir Lancelot fell down more than ten fathom into a cave full
of straw.

And then sir Meliagaunt departed and made no fare, no more than
he that wist not where he was. And when sir Lancelot was thus missed
they marvelled where he was becomen, and then the queen and many
of them deemed that he was departed, as he was wont to do, suddenly.
For sir Meliagaunt made suddenly to put on side sir Lavain's horse,
that they might all understand that sir Lancelot were departed suddenly.

So then it passed on till after dinner, and then sir Lavain would
not stint until he had horse-litters for the wounded knights, that they
might be carried in them. And so, with the queen, both ladies and
gentlewomen and other rode unto Westminster. And there the knights
told how sir Meliagaunt had appealed the queen of high treason, and
how sir Lancelot received the glove of him, 'and this day eight days
they shall do battle before you.'

'By my head,' said king Arthur, 'I am afeared sir Meliagaunt hath
charged himself with a great charge. But where is sir Lancelot?' said
the king. 'Sir we wot not where he is, but we deem he is ridden to some
adventure, as he is oftentimes wont to do, for he had sir Lavain's
horse.' 'Let him be,' said the king, 'for he will be founden but if he be
trapped with some treason.'

Thus leave we sir Lancelot lying within that cave in great pain.
And every day there came a lady and brought his meat and his drink,
and wooed him every day to have lain by her, and ever sir Lancelot
said her nay. Then said she, 'Sir, ye are not wise, for ye may never
out of this prison but if ye have my help. And also your lady, queen
Guenevere, shall be burnt in your default unless that ye be there at the
day of battle.'

'God defend,' said sir Lancelot, 'that she should be burnt in my default! And if it be so,' said sir Lancelot, 'that I may not be there, it shall be well understand, both at the king and the queen and with all men of worship, that I am dead, sick, other in prison. For all men that know me will say for me that I am in some evil case and I be not that day there. And thus well I understand that there is some good knight, other of my blood, other some other that loves me, that will take my quarrel in hand. And therefore,' said sir Lancelot, 'wit you well, ye shall not fear me, and if there were no mo women in all this land but ye, yet shall not I have ado with you.'

'Then are ye shamed,' said the lady, 'and destroyed for ever.'

'As for world's shame, now Jesu defend me! And as for my distress, it is welcome, whatsomever it be that God sends me.'

So she came to him again the same day that the battle should be and said, 'Sir Lancelot, bethink you, for ye are too hard-hearted. And therefore, and ye would but once kiss me, I should deliver you and your armour, and the best horse that was within sir Meliagaunt stable.'

'As for to kiss you,' said sir Lancelot, 'I may do that and lose no worship. And wit you well, and I understood there were any disworship for to kiss you, I would not do it.' And then he kissed her.

And anon she got him up until his armour, and when he was armed she brought him till a stable where stood twelve good coursers, and bade him to choose of the best. Then sir Lancelot looked upon a white courser and that liked him best, and anon he commanded the keepers fast to saddle him* with the best saddle of war that there was*, and so it was done as he bad.* Then he got his own spear in his hand and his sword by his side, and then he commended the lady unto God and said, 'Lady, for this day's deed I shall do you service, if ever it lie in my power.'

Now leave we here sir Lancelot, all that ever he might gallop, and speak we of queen Guenevere that was brought till a fire to be burnt. For sir Meliagaunt was sure, him thought, that sir Lancelot should not be at that battle, and therefore he ever cried upon sir Arthur to do him justice other else bring forth sir Lancelot.

Then was the king and all the court full sore abashed and shamed that the queen should have be burnt in the default of sir Lancelot. 'My lord, king Arthur,' said sir Lavain, 'ye may understand that it is not well with my lord sir Lancelot, for and he were on live, so he be not sick other in prison, wit you well he would have been here. For never heard ye that ever he failed yet his part for whom he should do battle for. And therefore,' said sir Lavain, 'my lord king Arthur, I beseech you that ye will give me licence to do battle here this day for my lord and master, and for to save my lady the queen.'

'Grauntmercy, gentle sir Lavain,' said king Arthur, 'for I dare say all that sir Meliagaunt putteth upon my lady the queen is wrong. For I have spoken with all the ten wounded knights, and there is not one of them, and he were whole and able to do battle, but he would prove upon sir Meliagaunt body that it is false that he putteth upon my lady.'

'And so shall I,' said sir Lavain, 'in the defence of my lord, sir Lancelot, and ye will give me leave.'

'And I give you leave,' said king Arthur, 'and do your best, for I dare well say there is some treason done to sir Lancelot.'

Then was sir Lavain armed and horsed, and deliverly at the list's end he rode to perform his battle. And right as the heralds should cry: 'Laissez les aller!' right so came sir Lancelot driving with all the might of his horse. And then king Arthur cried: 'Whoa!' and 'Abide!'

And then was sir Lancelot called on horseback* tofore king Arthur and there he told openly tofore the king all how that sir Meliagaunt had served him first and last. And when the king and queen and all the lords knew of the treason of sir Meliagaunt, they were all ashamed on his behalf. Then was the queen sent for and set by the king in the great trust of her champion.

And then there was no more else to say but* sir Lancelot and sir Meliagaunt dressed them unto battle, and took their spears and so they came togethers* as thunder, and there sir Lancelot bore him quite over his horse croup. And then sir Lancelot alight and dressed his shield on his shoulder and took his sword in his hand, and sir Meliagaunt in the same wise dressed him unto him, and there they* smote many great strokes together. And at the last sir Lancelot smote him such a buffet upon the helmet that he fell on the tone side to the earth. And then he cried upon him loud and said, 'Most noble knight, sir Lancelot, save my life! For I yield me unto you, and I require you, as ye be a knight and fellow of the Table Round, slay me not, for I yield me as overcomen, and whether I shall live or die, I put me in the king's hand and yours.'

Then sir Lancelot wist not what to do, for he had liefer than all the good in the world that he might be revenged upon him. So sir Lancelot looked upon the queen, if he might espy by any sign or countenance what she would have done. And anon the queen wagged her head upon sir Lancelot, as who saith, 'slay him.' And full well knew sir Lancelot by her signs that she would have him dead.

Then sir Lancelot bade him, 'Arise, for shame, and perform this battle with me to the utterance!'

'Nay,' said sir Meliagaunt, 'I will never arise until that ye take me as yolden and recreant.'

'Well, I shall proffer you a large proffer,' said sir Lancelot, 'that is for to say, I shall unarm my head and my left quarter of my body, all that may be unarmed as for that quarter, and I will let bind my left hand behind me there it shall not help me, and right so I shall do battle with you.'

Then sir Meliagaunt start up upon his legs and said on high* 'Take heed, my lord Arthur, of this proffer, for I will take it, and let him be disarmed and bounden according to his proffer.'

'What say ye?' said king Arthur unto sir Lancelot, 'Will ye abide by your proffer?'

'Yea, my lord,' said sir Lancelot, 'for I will never go from that I have once said.'

Then the knights parters of the field disarmed sir Lancelot, first his head and then his left arm and his left side, and they bound his left arm to his left side behind his back, without shield or anything. And anon they yode togethers. Wit you well there was many a lady and many a knight marvelled of sir Lancelot that would jeopardy himself in such wise.

Then sir Meliagaunt came with sword all on height, and sir Lancelot shewed him openly his bare head and the bare left side. And when he went to have smitten him upon the bare head, then lightly he devoided the left leg and the left side and put his right* hand and his sword to that stroke, and so put it on side with great sleight. And then with great force sir Lancelot smote him on the helmet such a buffet that the stroke carved the head in two parties.

Then there was no more to do, but he was drawn out of the field, and at the great instance of the knights of the Table Round the king suffered him to be interred, and the mention made upon him who slew him and for what cause he was slain.

And then the king and the queen made more of sir Lancelot, and more was he cherished than ever he was aforehand.

5. *The Healing of Sir Urry*

(Caxton XIX, 10–13)

Then, as the French book maketh mention, there was a good knight in the land of Hungary whose name was sir Urry. And he was an adventurous knight, and in all places where he might hear any adventurous deeds and of worship there would he be.

So it happened in Spain there was an earl, and his son's name was called sir Alpheus. And at a great tournament in Spain this sir Urry, knight of Hungary, and sir Alpheus of Spain encountered togethers for very envy, and so either undertook other to the utterance. And by fortune this sir Urry slew sir Alpheus, the earl's son of Spain. But this knight that was slain had given sir Urry, or ever he were slain, seven great wounds, three on the head and three on his body, and one upon his left hand. And this sir Alpheus had a mother which was a great sorceress, and she, for the despite of her son's death, wrought by her subtle crafts that sir Urry should never be whole, but ever his wounds should one time fester and another time bleed, so that he should never be whole until the best knight of the world had searched his wounds. And thus she made her avaunt, wherethrough it was known that this sir Urry should never be whole.

Then his mother let make an horse-litter and put him therein with two palfreys carrying him. And then she took with him his sister, a full fair damsel, whose name was Fileloly, and a page with them to keep their horses, and so they led sir Urry through many countries. For, as the French book saith, she led him so seven year thorough all lands christened and never could find no knight that might ease her son.

So she came unto Scotland and into the bounds of England. And by fortune she came unto the feast of Pentecost until king Arthur's court that at that time was holden at Carlisle. And when she came there she made it to be openly known how that she was come into that land for to heal her son. Then king Arthur let call that lady and ask her the cause why she brought that hurt knight into that land.

'My most noble king,' said that lady, 'wit you well I brought him hither to be healed of his wounds, that of all this seven year might never be whole.' And thus she told the king, and where he was wounded and with whom, and how his mother discovered it in her pride how she had wrought by enchantment that he should never be whole until the best knight of the world had searched his wounds.

'And so I have passed all the lands christened through to have him healed except this land, and if I fail here in this land I will never take more pain upon me. And that is great pity, for he was a good knight and of great noblesse.'

'What is his name?' said king Arthur.

'My good and gracious lord,' she said, 'his name is sir Urry of the Mount.'

'In good time,' said the king. 'And sithen ye are come into this land, ye are right welcome. And wit you well, here shall your son be healed and ever any Christian man may heal him. And for to give all other men of worship a courage, I myself will essay to handle your son, and so shall all the kings, dukes and earls that been here present at this time; not presuming upon me that I am so worthy to heal your son by my deeds, but I will courage other men of worship to do as I will do.'

And then the king commanded all the kings, dukes and earls and all noble knights of the Round Table that were there that time present to come into the meadow of Carlisle. And so at that time there were but an hundred and ten of the Round Table, for forty knights were that time away.

And so here we must begin at king Arthur, as is* kindly to begin at him that was that time the most man of worship christened. Then king Arthur looked upon sir Urry, and he thought he was a full likely man when he was whole. And then the king made to take him down off the litter and laid him upon the earth, and anon there was laid a cushion of gold that he should kneel upon. And then king Arthur said,

'Fair knight, me reweth of thy hurt, and for to courage all other knights I will pray thee softly to suffer me to handle thy wounds.'

'My most noble christened king, do ye as ye list,' said sir Urry, 'for I am at the mercy of God and at your commandment.'

So then king Arthur softly handled him. And then some of his wounds renewed upon bleeding. [*Then many kings, dukes and earls essayed and failed.*]

Then came in sir Gawain with his three sons . . . and all they failed. Then came in sir Agravain, sir Gaheris, and sir Mordred, and the good knight sir Gareth that was of very knighthood worth all the brethren.

So came in the knights of sir Lancelot's kin, but sir Lancelot was not that time in the court, for he was that time upon his adventures. . . All these were of sir Lancelot's kin, and all they failed.

[*Then came many others, as*] sir Lucan the Butler; sir Bedivere, his brother; sir Brandiles; sir Constantine, sir Cador's son of Cornwall that was king after Arthur's days; and sir Clegis; sir Priamus which was christened by the means of sir Tristram, the noble knight . . . sir Bellinger le Bewse that was son to the good knight sir Alexander le Orphelin that was slain by the treason of king Mark.

(Also that traitor slew the noble knight sir Tristram as he sat harping afore his lady, La Belle Isolde, with a trenchant glaive, for whose death was the most wailing of any knight that ever was in king Arthur's days, for there was never none so bewailed as was sir Tristram and sir Lamorak, for they were with treason slain; sir Tristram by king Mark, and sir Lamorak by sir Gawain and his brethren. And this sir Bellinger revenged the death of his father, sir Alexander, and sir Tristram, for he slew king Mark. And La Belle Isolde died swooning upon the cross of sir Tristram, whereof was great pity. And all that were with king Mark which were of assent of the death of sir Tristram were slain, as sir Andred and many other.)

Then came [*very many other good knights and*] all these hundred knights and ten searched sir Urry's wounds by the commandment of king Arthur.

'Mercy Jesu!' said king Arthur, 'where is sir Lancelot du Lake that he is not here at this time?' And thus as they stood and spoke of many things, there one espied sir Lancelot that came riding toward them, and anon they told the king. 'Peace,' said the king, 'let no man say nothing until he be come to us.' So when sir Lancelot had espied king Arthur he descended down from his horse and came to the king and salued him and them all.

And anon as the damsel, sir Urry's sister, saw sir Lancelot, she roamed to her brother thereas he lay in his litter and said, 'Brother, here is come a knight that my heart giveth greatly unto.' 'Fair sister,' said sir Urry, 'so doth my heart light greatly against him, and certainly I hope now to be healed for* my heart giveth unto him more* than to all these that hath searched me.'

Then said king Arthur unto sir Lancelot, 'Sir, ye must do as we have done,' and told him what they had done and shewed him them all that had searched him.

'Jesu defend me,' said sir Lancelot, 'while so many noble kings and knights have essayed and* failed, that I should presume upon me to achieve that all ye, my lords, might not achieve.'

'Ye shall not choose,' said king Arthur, 'for I command you to do as we all have done.'

'My most renowned lord,' said sir Lancelot, 'Ye* know well I dare not, nor may not, disobey you. But and I might or durst, wit you well I would not take upon me to touch that wounded knight in that intent that I should pass all other knights. Jesu defend me from that shame!'

'Sir, ye take it wrong,' said king Arthur, 'for ye shall not do it for no presumption, but for to bear us fellowship, insomuch as ye be a fellow of the Round Table. And wit you well,' said king Arthur, 'and ye prevail not and heal him, I dare say there is no knight in this land that may heal him. And therefore I pray you do as we have done.'

And then all the kings and knights for the most party prayed sir Lancelot to search him. And then the wounded knight, sir Urry, sat him up weakly and said unto sir Lancelot. 'Now courteous knight, I require thee, for God's sake, heal my wounds! For methinks ever sithen ye came here my wounds grieveth me not so much as they did.'

'Ah! my fair lord,' said sir Lancelot, 'Jesu would that I might help you! For I shame sore with myself that I should be thus required, for never was I able in worthiness to do so high a thing.'

Then sir Lancelot kneeled down by the wounded knight, saying, 'My lord Arthur, I must do your commandment, which is sore against my heart.' And then he held up his hands and looked unto the east, saying secretly unto himself, 'Now, blessed Father and Son and Holy Ghost, I beseech Thee of Thy mercy that my simple worship and honesty be saved, and Thou Blessed Trinity, Thou mayest give me power to heal this sick knight by the great virtue and grace of Thee, but, good Lord, never of myself.'

And then sir Lancelot prayed sir Urry to let him see his head. And then, devoutly kneeling, he ransacked the three wounds, that they bled a little. And forthwithal the wounds fair healed and seemed as they had been whole a seven year. And in like wise he searched his body of other three wounds, and they healed in like wise. And then the last of all he searched his hand, and anon it fair healed.

Then king Arthur and all the kings and knights kneeled down and gave thankings and loving unto God and unto His blessed Mother. And ever sir Lancelot wept, as he had been a child that had been beaten.

Then king Arthur let ravish priests and clerks in the most devoutest wise to bring in sir Urry into Carlisle with singing and loving to God. And when this was done the king let clothe him in rich manner, and then was there but few better made knights in all the court, for he was passingly well made and bigly.

Then king Arthur asked sir Urry how he felt himself.

'Ah! my good and gracious lord, I felt myself never so lusty.'

'Then will ye joust and do deeds of* arms?' said king Arthur.

'Sir, and I had all that longed unto jousts, I would be soon ready.'

Then king Arthur made a party of a hundred knights to be against an hundred, and so upon the morn they jousted for a diamond, but there jousted none of the dangerous knights. And so, for to shorten this tale, sir Urry and sir Lavain jousted best that day, for there was none of them but he overthrew and pulled down a thirty knights.

And then by assent of all the kings and lords sir Urry and sir Lavain were made knights of the Table Round. And then sir Lavain cast his love unto dame Fileloly, sir Urry sister. And then they were wedded with great joy, and so king Arthur gave to every of them a barony of lands.

And this sir Urry would never go from sir Lancelot, but he and sir Lavain awaited evermore upon him. And they were in all the court accounted for good knights and full desirous in arms. And many noble deeds they did, for they would have no rest but ever sought upon their deeds. Thus they lived in all that court with great noblesse and joy long times.

But every night and day sir Agravain, sir Gawain's brother, awaited queen Guenevere and sir Lancelot to put them both to a rebuke and a shame.

And so I leave here of this tale, and overleap great books of sir Lancelot, what great adventures he did when he was called 'le Chevalier de

Chariot.' For, as the French book saith, because of despite that knights and ladies called him 'the Knight that rode in the Chariot,' like as he were judged to the gibbet, therefore, in the despite of all them that named him so, he was carried in a chariot a twelve-month; for but little after that he had slain sir Meliagaunt in the queen's quarrel, he never of a twelve-month came on horseback. And, as the French book saith, he did that twelve month more than forty battles.

And because I have lost the very matter of Chevalier de Chariot I depart from the tale of sir Lancelot; and here I go unto the Morte Arthur, and that caused sir Agravain.

And here on the other side followeth the most piteous tale of the Morte Arthur Sans Guerdon par le chevalier sir Thomas Malory, knight. Jesu, aide lui pour votre bonne merci! Amen.

PART EIGHT

THE MORTE ARTHUR

1. Slander and Strife

(Caxton XX, 1–8)

In May, when every heart flourisheth and burgeoneth (for, as the season is lusty to behold and comfortable, so man and woman rejoiceth and gladdeth of summer coming with his fresh flowers, for winter with his rough winds and blasts causeth lusty men and women to cower and to sit by fires), so this season it befell in the month of May a great anger and unhap that stinted not till the flower of chivalry of all the world was destroyed and slain.

And all was long upon two unhappy knights which were named sir Agravain and sir Mordred, that were brethren unto sir Gawain. For this sir Agravain and sir Mordred had ever a privy hate unto the queen, dame Guenevere, and to sir Lancelot; and daily and nightly they ever watched upon sir Lancelot. So it misfortuned sir Gawain and all his brethren were in king Arthur's chamber, and then sir Agravain said thus openly, and not in no counsel, that many knights might hear: 'I marvel that we all be not ashamed both to see and to know how sir Lancelot lieth daily and nightly by the queen. And all we know well that it is so, and it is shamefully suffered of us all that we should suffer so noble a king as king Arthur is to be shamed.'

Then spoke sir Gawain and said, 'Brother, sir Agravain, I pray you and charge you, move no such matters no more afore me, for wit you well, I will not be of your counsel.'

'So God me help,' said sir Gaheris and sir Gareth, 'we will not be known of your deeds.'

'Then will I!' said sir Mordred.

'I lieve you well,' said sir Gawain, 'for ever unto all unhappiness, sir, ye will grant. And I would that ye left all this and make you not so busy, for I know,' said sir Gawain, 'what will fall of it.'

'Fall whatsomever fall may,' said sir Agravain, 'I will disclose it to the king!'

'Not by my counsel,' said sir Gawain, 'for, and there arise war and wrack betwixt sir Lancelot and us, wit you well, brother, there will

many kings and great lords hold with sir Lancelot. Also, brother
sir Agravain', said sir Gawain, 'ye must remember how oftentimes
sir Lancelot hath rescued the king and the queen; and the best of us
all had been full cold at the heart-root had not sir Lancelot been
better than we, and that hath he proved himself full oft. And as for
my part,' said sir Gawain, 'I will never be against sir Lancelot for one
day's deed; that was when he rescued me from king Carados of the
Dolorous Tower, and slew him and saved my life. Also, brother sir
Agravain and sir Mordred, in like wise sir Lancelot rescued you
both and three score and two from sir Tarquin. And therefore,
brother, methinks such noble deeds and kindness should be remem-
bered.'

'Do as ye list,' said sir Agravain, 'for I will lain it no longer.'

So with these words came in sir Arthur.

'Now, brother,' said sir Gawain, 'stint your strife.'

'That will I not,' said sir Agravain and sir Mordred.

'Well, will ye so?' said sir Gawain. 'Then God speed you, for I will
not hear of your tales nother be of your council.'

'No more will I,' said sir Gaheris.

'Nother I,' said sir Gareth, 'for I shall never say evil by that man
that made me knight.'

And therewithal they three departed making great dole. 'Alas!' said
sir Gawain and sir Gareth, 'now is this realm wholly destroyed and
mischieved, and the noble fellowship of the Round Table shall be
disparbeled.'

So they departed, and then king Arthur asked them what noise they
made. 'My lord,' said sir Agravain, 'I shall tell you, for I may keep it
no longer. Here is I and my brother sir Mordred broke unto my
brother sir Gawain, sir Gaheris and to sir Gareth; for this is all, to make
it short: we know all that sir Lancelot holdeth your queen, and hath
done long, and we be your sister's sons, we may suffer it no longer.
And all we wot that ye should be above sir Lancelot, and ye are the
king that made him knight, and therefore we will prove it that he is
a traitor to your person.'

'If it be so,' said the king, 'wit you well, he is none other. But I
would be loth to begin such a thing but I might have proofs of it, for
sir Lancelot is an hardy knight, and all ye know that he is the best
knight among us all, and but if he be taken with the deed he will

fight with him that bringeth up the noise, and I know no knight that is able to match him. Therefore, and it be soth as ye say, I would that he were taken with the deed.'

For, as the French book saith, the king was full loth that such a noise should be upon sir Lancelot and his queen; for the king had a deeming of it, but he would not hear thereof, for sir Lancelot had done so much for him and for the queen so many times that wit you well the king loved him passingly well.

'My lord,' said sir Agravain, 'ye shall ride to-morrow an-hunting, and doubt ye not, sir Lancelot will not go with you. And so when it draweth toward night ye may send the queen word that ye will lie out all that night, and so may ye send for your cooks. And then, upon pain of death, that night we shall take him with the queen, and we shall bring him unto you, quick or dead.'

'I will well,' said the king. 'Then I counsel you to take with you sure fellowship.'

'Sir,' said sir Agravain, 'my brother sir Mordred and I will take with us twelve knights of the Round Table.'

'Beware,' said king Arthur, 'for I warn you, ye shall find him wight.'

'Let us deal!' said sir Agravain and sir Mordred.

So on the morn king Arthur rode an-hunting and sent word to the queen that he would be out all that night. Then sir Agravain and sir Mordred got to them twelve knights and hid themself in a chamber in the castle of Carlisle. And these were their names, sir Collgrevaunce, sir Mador le la Porte, sir Gingaline, sir Meliot de Logres, sir Petipace of Winchelsea, sir Galleron of Galloway, sir Melion de la Mountain, sir Ascomore, sir Gromoresom Erioure, sir Cursesalain, sir Florence, and sir Lovel. So these twelve knights were with sir Mordred and sir Agravain, and all they were of Scotland, other else of sir Gawain's kin, other well-willers to his brother.

So when the night came sir Lancelot told sir Bors how he would go that night and speak with the queen. 'Sir,' said sir Bors, 'ye shall not go this night by my counsel.' 'Why?' said sir Lancelot. 'Sir, for I dread me ever of sir Agravain that waiteth upon you daily to do you shame and us all. And never gave my heart against no going that ever ye went to the queen so much as now, for I mistrust that the king is out this night from the queen because peradventure he hath lain some watch for you and the queen. Therefore I dread me sore of some treason.' 'Have ye no dread,' said sir Lancelot, 'for I shall go and come again and make no tarrying.' 'Sir,' said sir Bors, 'that me repents, for I dread me sore that your going this night shall wrath us all.' 'Fair nephew,' said sir Lancelot, 'I marvel me much why ye say thus, sithen the queen hath sent for me. And wit you well, I will not be so much a coward, but she shall understand I will see her good grace.' 'God speed you well,' said sir Bors, 'and send you sound and safe again!'

So sir Lancelot departed and took his sword under his arm, and so he walked in his mantle, that noble knight, and put himself in great jeopardy. And so he passed on till he came to the queen's chamber, and so lightly he was had into the chamber. For, as the French book saith, the queen and sir Lancelot were togethers. And whether they were abed other at other manner of disports, me list not thereof make no mention, for love that time was not as love is nowadays.

But thus as they were together there came sir Agravain and sir Mordred with twelve knights with them of the Round Table, and they said with great crying and scaring voice,

"Thou traitor, sir Lancelot, now are thou taken!'

And thus they cried with a loud voice, that all the court might hear it. And these fourteen knights all were armed at all points, as they should fight in a battle.

'Alas!' said queen Guenevere, 'now are we mischieved both!'

'Madam,' said sir Lancelot, 'is there here any armour within your chamber* that might cover my poor* body withal? And if there be any, give it me and I shall soon stint their malice, by the grace of God!'

'Now, truly,' said the queen, 'I have none armour nother helm, shield, sword, nother spear; wherefore I dread me sore our long love is come to a mischievous end. For I hear by their noise there be many noble knights, and well I wot they be surely armed, and against them ye may make no resistance. Wherefore ye are likely to be slain, and then shall I be burnt! For and ye might escape them,' said the queen, 'I would not doubt but that ye would rescue me in what danger that I ever stood in.'

'Alas!' said sir Lancelot, 'in all my life thus was I never bestead that I should be thus shamefully slain, for lack of mine armour.'

But ever in one* sir Agravain and sir Mordred cried, 'Traitor knight, come out of the queen's chamber!' For wit thou well thou art beset so that thou shalt not escape.'

'Ah! Jesu mercy!' said sir Lancelot, 'this shameful cry and noise I may not suffer, for better were death at once than thus to endure this pain.'

Then he took the queen in his arms and kissed her and said, 'Most noblest Christian queen, I beseech you, as ye have been ever my special good lady, and I at all times your poor knight and true unto my power, and as I never failed you in right nor in wrong sithen the first day king Arthur made me knight, that ye will pray for my soul if that I be slain. For well I am assured that sir Bors, my nephew, and all the remnant of my kin, with sir Lavain and sir Urry, that they will not fail you to rescue you from the fire. And therefore, mine own lady, recomfort yourself, whatsomever come of me, that ye go with sir Bors, my nephew, and sir Urry and* they all will do you all the pleasure that they can or* may, and ye shall live like a queen upon my lands.'

'Nay, sir Lancelot, nay!' said the queen. 'Wit thou well that I will never* live long after thy days. But and ye be slain I will take my death as meekly as ever did martyr take his death for Jesu Christ's sake.'

'Well, madam,' said sir Lancelot, 'sith it is so that the day is come that our love must depart, wit you well I shall sell my life as dear as I may. And a thousandfold,' said sir Lancelot, 'I am more heavier for you than for myself! And now I had liefer than to be lord of all Christendom that I had sure armour upon me, that men might speak of my deeds or ever I were slain.'

'Truly,' said the queen, 'and it might please God, I would that they would take me and slay me and suffer you to escape.'

'That shall never be,' said sir Lancelot, 'God defend me from such a shame! But Jesu Christ, be Thou my shield and mine armour!'

And therewith sir Lancelot wrapped his mantle about his arm well and surely. And by then they had gotten a great form out of the hall, and therewith they all rushed at the door.

'Now, fair lords,' said sir Lancelot, 'leave your noise and your rushing, and I shall set open this door, and then may ye do with me what it liketh you.'

'Come off, then,' said they all, 'and do it, for it availeth thee not to strive against us all! And therefore let us into this chamber, and we shall save thy life until thou come to king Arthur.'

Then sir Lancelot unbarred the door, and with his left hand he held it open a little, that but one man might come in at once. And so there came striding a good knight, a much man and a large, and his name was called sir Collgrevaunce of Gore. And he with a sword struck at sir Lancelot mightily, and so he put aside the stroke, and gave him such a buffet upon the helmet that he fell grovelling dead within the chamber door. Then sir Lancelot with great might drew that dead knight* within the chamber door, and then sir Lancelot, with help of the queen and her ladies, he was lightly armed in Collgrevaunce armour.

And ever stood sir Agravain and sir Mordred, crying, 'Traitor knight! Come forth out of the queen's chamber!'

'Sirs, leave your noise,' said sir Lancelot, 'for wit you well, sir Agravain, ye shall not prison me this night! And therefore, and ye do by my counsel, go ye all from this chamber door and make you no such crying and such manner of slander as ye do. For I promise you by my knighthood, and ye will depart and make no more noise, I shall as to-morn appear afore you all and before the king, and then let it be seen which of you all, other else ye all, that will depreve me of treason. And there shall I answer you, as a knight should, that hither I came to the queen for no manner of mal engine, and that will I prove and make it good upon you with my hands.'

'Fie upon thee, traitor,' said sir Agravain and sir Mordred, 'for we will have thee maugre thine head, and slay thee, and we list! For we let thee wit we have the choice of king Arthur to save thee other slay thee.'

'Ah! sirs,' said sir Lancelot, 'is there none other grace with you? Then keep yourself!'

And then sir Lancelot set all open the chamber door, and mightily and knightly he strode in among them. And anon at the first stroke he slew sir Agravain, and anon after twelve of his fellows. Within a while he had laid them down cold to the earth, for there was none of the twelve knights might stand sir Lancelot one buffet. And also he wounded sir Mordred, and therwithal he fled with all his might.

And then sir Lancelot returned again unto the queen and said, 'Madam, now wit you well, all our true love is brought to an end, for now will king Arthur ever be my foe. And therefore, madam, and it like you that I may have you with me, I shall save you from all manner adventures dangers.'

'Sir, that is not best,' said the queen, 'meseemeth, for now ye have done so much harm it will be best that ye hold you still with this.

And if ye see that as to-morn they will put me unto death, then may ye rescue me as ye think best.'

'I will well,' said sir Lancelot, 'for have ye no doubt, while I am a man living I shall rescue you.' And then he kissed her, and either of them gave other a ring, and so the queen he left there and went until his lodging.

When sir Bors saw sir Lancelot he was never so glad of his home-coming as he was then.* 'Jesu mercy!' said sir Lancelot, 'why be ye all armed? What meaneth this?'

'Sir,' said sir Bors, 'after ye were departed from us we all that been of your blood and your well-willers were so adretched that some of us lep out of our beds naked, and some in their dreams caught naked swords in their hands. And therefore,' said sir Bors, 'we deemed there was some great strife on hand, and so we deemed that we were betrapped with some treason; and therefore we made us thus ready, what need that ever ye were in.'

'My fair nephew,' said sir Lancelot unto sir Bors, 'now shall ye wit all that this night I was more hard bestead than ever I was days of my life. And thanked be God, I am myself escaped their danger.' And so he told them all how and in what manner, as ye have heard toforehand. 'And therefore, my fellows,' said sir Lancelot, 'I pray you all that ye will be of heart good, and help me in what need that ever I stand, for now is war comen to us all.'

'Sir,' said sir Bors, 'all is welcome that God sendeth us, and as we have taken much weal with you and much worship, we will take the woe with you as we have taken the weal.'

And therefore they said, all the good knights, 'Look ye take no discomfort! For there is no bands of knights under heaven but we shall be able to grieve them as much as they us, and therefore discomfort not yourself by no manner. And we shall gather together all that we love and that loveth us, and what that ye will have done shall be done. And therefore, sir Lancelot,' said they, 'we will take the woe with the weal'.*

'Grauntmercy,' said sir Lancelot, 'of your good comfort, for in my great distress, fair nephew, ye comfort me greatly, and much I am beholding unto you.* But this, my fair nephew, I would that ye did, in all haste that ye may, or it is far days past: that ye will look in their lodging that been lodged nigh here about the king, which will hold with me and which will not. For now I would know which were my friends from my foes.'

'Sir,' said sir Bors, 'I shall do my pain, and or it be seven of the clock I shall wit of such as ye have doubt for, who that will hold with you.'

Then sir Bors called unto him sir Lionel, sir Ector de Maris, sir Blamour de Ganis, sir Bleoberis de Ganis, sir Gahalantine, sir Galihodin, sir Galihud, sir Menaduke, sir Villiers the Valiaunt, sir Hebes le Renown, sir Lavain, sir Urry of Hungary, sir Neroveus, sir Plenorius (for these two were knights that sir Lancelot won upon a bridge, and therefore they would never be against him,) and sir Harry le Fitz Lake, and sir Selises of the Dolorous Tower, sir Melias de Lile, and sir Bellinger le Bewse that was sir Alexander le Orphelin son (because his mother was Alice la Belle Pelerin, and she was kin unto sir Lancelot, he held with him.) So came sir Palomides and sir Saphir, his brother; sir Clegis, sir Sadok, sir Dinas and sir Clarrius of Cleremont.

So these two-and-twenty knights drew them togethers, and by then they were armed and on horseback they promised sir Lancelot to do what he would. Then there fell to them, what of North Wales and of Cornwall, for sir Lamorak's sake and for sir Tristram's sake, to the number of a seven score knights.

Then spoke sir Lancelot: 'Wit you well, I have been ever since I came to this court well-willed unto my lord Arthur and unto my lady queen Guenevere unto my power. And this night because my lady the queen sent for me to speak with her, I suppose it was made by treason; howbeit I dare largely excuse her person, notwithstanding I was there by a forecast nearhand slain; but as Jesu provided me I escaped all their malice and treason'* And then that noble knight sir Lancelot told them how he was hard bestead in the queen's chamber, and how and in what manner he escaped from them.

'And therefore wit you well, my fair lords, I am sure there nis but war unto me and to mine. And for cause I have slain this night sir Agravain, sir Gawain's brother, and at the least twelve of his fellows, and for this cause now am I sure of mortal war. For these knights were sent by king Arthur to betray me, and therefore the king will in this heat and malice judge the queen unto burning, and that may not I suffer, that she should be burnt for my sake. For and I may be heard and suffered and so taken, I will fight for the queen, that she is a true lady until her lord. But the king in his heat, I dread, will not take me as I ought to be taken.'

'My lord, sir Lancelot,' said sir Bors, 'by mine advice, ye shall take the woe with the weal and take it in patience and thank God of it.* And sithen it is fallen as it is, I counsel you to keep yourself, for and ye will yourself there is no fellowship of knights christened that shall do you wrong. And also I will counsel you, my lord, that my lady queen Guenevere, and she be in any distress, insomuch as she is in pain for your sake, that ye knightly rescue her; for and ye did any other wise all the world would speak of* you shame to the world's end. Insomuch as ye were taken with her, whether ye did right other wrong, it is now your part to hold with the queen, that she be not slain and put to a mischievous death. For and she so die, the shame shall be evermore yours.'

'Now Jesu defend me from shame,' said sir Lancelot, 'and keep and save my lady the queen from villainy and shameful death, and that she never be destroyed in my default! Wherefore, my fair lords, my kin and my friends,' said sir Lancelot, 'what will ye do?'

And anon they said all with one voice, 'We will do as ye will do.'

'Then I put this case unto you,' said sir Lancelot, 'that my lord, king Arthur, by evil counsel will to-morn in his heat put my lady the queen unto the fire and there to be burnt. Then, I pray you, counsel me what is best for me to do.'

Then they said all at once with one voice:

'Sir, us thinks best that ye knightly rescue the queen. Insomuch as she shall be burnt, it is for your sake; and it is to suppose, and ye might be handled, ye should have the same death, other else a more shamefuller death. And, sir, we say all that ye have rescued her from death many times for other men's quarrels; therefore us seemeth it is more your worship that ye rescue the queen from this peril,* insomuch that she hath it for your sake.'

Then sir Lancelot stood still and said, 'My fair lords, wit you well I would be loth to do that thing that should dishonour you or my blood; and wit you well I would be full loth that my lady the queen should die such a shameful death. But and it be so that ye will counsel me to rescue her, I must do much harm or I rescue her, and peradventure I shall there destroy some of my best friends, and that should much repent me. And peradventure there be some, and they could well bring it about or disobey my lord king Arthur, they would soon come to me, the which I were loth to hurt. And if so be that I may win the queen away, where shall I keep her?'

'Sir, that shall be the least care of us all,' said sir Bors, 'for how did the most noble knight sir Tristram? By your good will, kept not he with him La Belle Isolde near three year in Joyous Gard, the which was done by your althers advice? And that same place is your own, and in like wise may ye do, and ye list, and take the queen knightly away with you, if so be that the king will judge her to be burnt. And in Joyous Gard may ye keep her long enough until the heat be past of the king, and then it may fortune you to bring the queen again to the king with great worship, and peradventure ye shall have then thank for her bringing home, and love and thank where other shall* have malgré.'

'That is hard for to do,' said sir Lancelot, 'for by sir Tristram I may have a warning: for when by means of treaties sir Tristram brought again La Belle Isolde unto king Mark from Joyous Gard, look ye now what fell on the end, how shamefully that false traitor king Mark slew him as he sat harping afore his lady, La Belle Isolde. With a grounden glaive he thrust him in behind to the heart, which grieveth sore me,' said sir Lancelot, 'to speak of his death, for all the world may not find such another knight.'

'All this is truth,' said sir Bors, 'but there is one thing shall courage you and us all: ye know well that king Arthur and king Mark were never like of conditions, for there was never yet man that ever could prove king Arthur untrue of his promise.'

But so, to make short tale, they were all condescended that, for better other for worse, if so were that the queen were brought on that morn to the fire, shortly they all would rescue her. And so by the advice of sir Lancelot they put them all in a bushment in a wood as nigh Carlisle as they might, and there they abode still to wit what the king would do.

Now turn we again unto sir Mordred that when* he was escaped from sir Lancelot he got his horse and mounted upon him and rode unto* king Arthur sore wounded and all forbled, and there he told the king all how it was, and how they were all slain save himself alone.

'Ah! Jesu, mercy! How may this be?' said the king. 'Took ye him in the queen's chamber?'

'Yea, so God me help,' said sir Mordred, 'there we found him unarmed, and anon he slew sir Collgrevaunce and armed him in his armour.' And so he told the king from the beginning to the ending.

'Jesu mercy!' said the king, 'he is a marvellous knight of prowess. And alas,' said the king, 'me sore repenteth that ever sir Lancelot should be against me, for now I am sure the noble fellowship of the Round Table is broken for ever, for with him will many a noble knight hold. And now it is fallen so,' said the king, 'that I may not with my worship but my queen must suffer death,' and was sore amoved.

So then there was made great ordinance in this ire, and the queen must needs be judged to the death. And the law was such in tho days that whatsomever they were, of what estate or degree, if they were founden guilty of treason there should be none other remedy but death, and other the menour other the taking with the deed should be causer of their hasty judgement. And right so was it ordained for queen Guenevere; because sir Mordred was escaped sore wounded, and the death of thirteen knights of the Round Table, these proofs and experiences caused king Arthur to command the queen to the fire and there to be burnt.

Then spoke sir Gawain and said,

'My lord Arthur, I would counsel you not to be over hasty, but that ye would put it in respite, this judgement of my lady the queen, for many causes. One is this, though it were so that sir Lancelot were found in the queen's chamber, yet it might be so that he came thither for none evil. For ye know, my lord,' said sir Gawain, 'that my lady the queen hath oftentimes been greatly beholden unto sir Lancelot, more than to any other knight; for oftentimes he hath saved her life and done battle for her when all the court refused the queen. And peradventure she sent for him for goodness and for none evil, to reward him for his good deeds that he had done to her in times past. And peradventure my lady the queen sent for him to that intent, that sir Lancelot should a come privily to her, weening that it had be best in eschewing of slander; for oftentimes we do many things that we ween for the best be, and yet peradventure it turneth to the worst. For I dare say,' said sir Gawain, 'my lady, your queen, is to you both good and true. And as for sir Lancelot, I dare say he will make it good upon any knight living that will put upon him villainy or shame, and in like wise he will make good for my lady the queen.'

'That I believe well,' said king Arthur, 'but I will not that way work with sir Lancelot, for he trusteth so much upon his hands and his might that he doubteth no man. And therefore for my queen he shall nevermore fight, for she shall have the law. And if I may get sir Lancelot, wit you well he shall have as shameful a death.'

'Jesu defend me,' said sir Gawain, 'that I never see it nor know it.'

'Why say you so?' said king Arthur, 'For perdé, ye have no cause to love him! For this night last past he slew your brother sir Agravain, a full good knight, and almost he had slain your other brother, sir Mordred, and also there he slew thirteen noble knights. And also remember you, sir Gawain, he slew two sons of yours, sir Florence and sir Lovel.'

'My lord,' said sir Gawain, 'of all this I have a knowledge, which of their deaths sore repents me. But insomuch as I gave them warning and told my brother and my sons aforehand what would fall on the end, and insomuch as they would not do by my counsel, I will not meddle me thereof, nor revenge me nothing of their deaths; for I told them there was no boot to strive with sir Lancelot. Howbeit I am sorry of the death of my brother and of my two sons, but they are the causers of their own death; for oftentimes I warned my brother sir Agravain, and I told him of the perils the which been now fallen.'

Then said king Arthur unto sir Gawain, 'Dear nephew, I pray you make* you ready, in your best armour, with your brethren, sir Gaheris and sir Gareth, to bring my queen to the fire and there to have her judgement and receive the death.'*

'Nay, my most noble king,' said sir Gawain, 'that will I never do, for wit you well I will never be in that place where so noble a queen as is my lady dame Guenevere shall take such a shameful end. For wit you well,' said sir Gawain, 'my heart will not serve me for to see her die, and it shall never be said that ever I was of your counsel for her death.'

'Then,' said the king unto sir Gawain, 'suffer your brethren sir Gaheris and sir Gareth to be there.' 'My lord,' said sir Gawain, 'wit you well they will be loth to be there present because of many adventures that is like to fall, but they are young and full unable to say you nay.'

Then spake sir Gaheris and the good knight sir Gareth unto king

Arthur: 'Sir, ye may well command us to be there, but wit you well it shall be sore against our will. But and we be there by your strait commandment, ye shall plainly hold us there excused. We will be there in peaceable wise, and bear none harness of war upon us.'

'In the name of God,' said the king, 'then make you ready, for she shall have soon her judgement.'

'Alas,' said sir Gawain, 'that ever I should endure to see this woeful day!' So sir Gawain turned him and wept heartily, and so he went into his chamber. And so the queen was led forth without Carlisle, and anon she was despoiled into her smock. And then her ghostly father was brought to her to be shriven of her misdeeds. Then was there weeping and wailing and wringing of hands of many lords and ladies; but there were but few in comparison that would bear any armour for to strength the death of the queen.

Then was there one that sir Lancelot had sent unto that place, which went to espy what time the queen should go unto her death. And anon as he saw the queen despoiled into her smock and shriven, then he gave sir Lancelot warning anon. Then was there but spurring and plucking up of horse, and right so they came unto the fire. And who that stood against them, there were they slain; there might none withstand sir Lancelot. So all that bore arms and withstood them, there were they slain, full many a noble knight. For there was slain sir Bellias le Orgulus, sir Segwarides, sir Grifflet, sir Brandiles, sir Aglovale, sir Tor; sir Walter, sir Gillimer, sir Reynold, (three brothers), and sir Damas, sir Priamus, sir Kay le Strange, sir Driant, sir Lambegus, sir Hermind; sir Pertolip, sir Perimones, (two brethren which were called the Green Knight and the Red Knight.)

And so in this rushing and hurling, as sir Lancelot thrang here and there, it misfortuned him to slay sir Gaheris and sir Gareth, the noble knight, for they were unarmed and unwares. As the French book saith, sir Lancelot smote sir Gaheris and sir Gareth upon the brain-pans, wherethrough that they were slain in the field. Howbeit in very truth sir Lancelot saw them not. And so were they found dead among the thickest of the press.

Then sir Lancelot, when he had thus done, and slain and put to flight all that would withstand him, then he rode straight unto queen Guenevere and made cast a kirtle and a gown upon her, and then he made her to be set behind him and prayed her to be of good cheer.

Now wit you well the queen was glad that she was at that time escaped from the death, and then she thanked God and sir Lancelot.

And so he rode his way with the queen, as the French book saith, unto Joyous Gard, and there he kept her as a noble knight should. And many great lords and some kings sent sir Lancelot* many good knights, and many full noble knights drew unto him. When this was known openly* that king Arthur and sir Lancelot were at debate many knights were glad, and many were sorry of their debate.

2. The Vengeance of sir Gawain

(Caxton XX, 9–18)

Now turn we again unto king Arthur, that when it was told him how and in what manner the queen was taken away from the fire, and when he heard of the death of his noble knights, and in especial sir Gaheris and sir Gareth, then he swooned for very pure sorrow. And when he awoke of his swough then he said, 'Alas, that ever I bore crown upon my head! For now have I lost the fairest fellowship of noble knights that ever held Christian king togethers. Alas, my good knights be slain and gone away from me, that now within this two days I have lost nigh forty knights and also the noble fellowship of sir Lancelot and his blood, for now I may nevermore hold them togethers with my worship. Now, alas! that ever this war began!

'Now, fair fellows,' said the king, 'I charge you that no man tell sir Gawain of the death of his two brethren, for I am sure,' said the king, 'when he heareth tell that sir Gareth is dead, he will go nigh out of his mind. Mercy Jesu!' said the king, 'why slew he sir Gaheris and sir Gareth? For I dare say, as for sir Gareth, he loved sir Lancelot of all men earthly.'

'That is truth,' said some knights, 'but they were slain in the hurling, as sir Lancelot thrang in the thickest of the press. And as they were unarmed, he smote them and wist not whom that he smote, and so unhappily they were slain.'

'Well,' said Arthur, 'the death of them will cause the greatest mortal war that ever was, for I am sure that when sir Gawain knoweth hereof that sir Gareth is slain, I shall never have rest of him till I have destroyed sir Lancelot's kin and himself both, other else he to destroy me. And therefore,' said the king, 'wit you well, my heart was never so heavy as it is now. And much more I am sorrier for my good knights' loss than for the loss of my fair queen; for queens I might have enough, but such a fellowship of good knights shall never be togethers in no company. And now I dare say,' said king Arthur, 'there was never Christian king that ever held such a fellowship togethers. And alas, that ever sir Lancelot and I should be at debate! Ah! Agravain, Agravain!' said the king, 'Jesu forgive it thy soul, for thine evil will that thou haddest and sir Mordred, thy brother, unto sir Lancelot hath caused all this sorrow.' And ever among these complaints the king wept and swooned.

Then came there one to sir Gawain and told him how the queen was led away with sir Lancelot, and nigh a four-and-twenty knights slain. 'Ah! Jesu, save me my two brethren!' said sir Gawain, 'For full well wist I,' said sir Gawain, 'that sir Lancelot would rescue her, other else he would die in that field. And to say the truth he were not of worship but if he had rescued the queen, insomuch as she should have be burnt for his sake. And as in that,' said sir Gawain, 'he hath done but knightly, and as I would have done myself and I had stand in like case. But where are my brethren?' said sir Gawain, 'I marvel that I see not of them.'

Then said that man, 'Truly, sir Gaheris and sir Gareth be slain.'

'Jesu defend!' said sir Gawain. 'For all this world I would not that they were slain, and in especial my good brother sir Gareth.'

'Sir,' said the man, 'he is slain, and that is great pity.'

'Who slew him?' said sir Gawain.

'Sir Lancelot,' said the man, 'slew them both.'

'That may I not believe,' said sir Gawain, 'that ever he slew my good brother sir Gareth, for I dare say, my brother loved him better than me and all his brethren and the king both. Also I dare say, and sir Lancelot had desired my brother sir Gareth with him, he would have been with him against the king and us all. And therefore I may never believe that sir Lancelot slew my brethren.'

'Verily, sir,' said the man, 'it is noised that he slew him.'

'Alas,' said sir Gawain, 'now is my joy gone!'

And then he fell down and swooned, and long he lay there as he had been dead. And when he arose out of his swough he cried out sorrowfully and said, 'Alas!'

And forthwith he ran unto the king, crying and weeping, and said, 'Ah! mine uncle, king Arthur! My good brother sir Gareth is slain, and so is my brother sir Gaheris, which were two noble knights.' Then the king wept and he both, and so they fell on swooning. And when they were revived, then spoke sir Gawain and said, 'Sir, I will go and see my brother sir Gareth.' 'Sir, ye may not see him,' said the king, 'for I caused him to be interred and sir Gaheris both, for I well understood that ye would make overmuch sorrow, and the sight of sir Gareth should have caused your double sorrow.'

'Alas, my lord,' said sir Gawain, 'how slew he my brother sir Gareth? I pray you tell me.' 'Truly,' said the king, 'I shall tell you as it hath been told me: sir Lancelot slew him and sir Gaheris both.' 'Alas,' said sir Gawain, 'they bore none arms against him, neither of them both.' 'I wot not how it was,' said the king, 'but as it is said, sir Lancelot slew them in the thickest of the* press and knew them not. And therefore let us shape a remedy for to revenge their deaths.'

'My king, my lord, and mine uncle,' said sir Gawain, 'wit you well, now I shall make you a promise which I shall hold by my knighthood, that from this day forward I shall never fail sir Lancelot until that one of us have slain that other. And therefore I require you, my lord and king, dress you unto the war, for wit you well, I will be revenged upon sir Lancelot; and therefore, as ye will have my service and my love, now haste you thereto and assay your friends. For I promise unto God,' said sir Gawain, 'for the death of my brother, sir Gareth, I shall seek sir Lancelot throughout seven king's realms, but I shall slay him, other else he shall slay me.'

'Sir, ye shall not need to seek him so far,' said the king, 'for as I hear say, sir Lancelot will abide me and us all within the castle of Joyous Gard. And much people draweth unto him, as I hear say.'

'That may I right well believe,' said sir Gawain; 'but, my lord,' he said, 'assay your friends and I will assay mine.'

'It shall be done,' said the king, 'and as I suppose I shall be big enough to drive him out of the biggest tower of his castle.'

So then the king sent letters and writs throughout all England, both the length and the breadth, for to assummon all his knights. And so unto king Arthur drew many knights, dukes, and earls, that he had a great host, and when they were assembled the king informed them how sir Lancelot had bereft him his queen. Then the king and all his host made them ready to lay siege about sir Lancelot where he lay within Joyous Gard.

And anon sir Lancelot heard thereof and purveyed him of many good knights; for with him held many knights, some for his own sake and some for the queen's sake. Thus they were on both parties well furnished and garnished of all manner of thing that longed unto the war. But king Arthur's host was so great that sir Lancelot's host would not abide him in the field. For he was full loth to do battle against the king; but sir Lancelot drew him unto his strong castle with all manner of victual plenty, and as many noble men as he might suffice within the town and the castle.

Then came king Arthur with sir Gawain with a great host and laid siege all about Joyous Gard, both the town and the castle. And there they made strong war on both parties, but in no wise sir Lancelot would ride out of the castle of long time; and nother he would not suffer none of his good knights to issue out, nother of the town nother of the castle, until fifteen weeks were past.

So it fell upon a day in harvest time that sir Lancelot looked over the walls and spoke on height unto king Arthur and to sir Gawain:

'My lords both, wit you well all this is in vain that ye make at this siege, for here win ye no worship, but malgré and dishonour. For and it list me to come myself out and my good knights, I should full soon make an end of this war.'

'Come forth,' said king Arthur unto sir Lancelot, 'and thou durst, and I promise thee I shall meet thee in mids of this field.'

'God defend me,' said sir Lancelot, 'that ever I should encounter with the most noble king that made me knight.'

'Now, fie upon thy fair language!' said the king, 'for wit thou well and trust it, I am thy mortal foe and ever will to my death-day; for thou hast slain my good knights and full noble men of my blood, that shall I never recover again. Also thou hast lain by my queen and holden her many winters, and sithen, like a traitor, taken her away from me by force.'

'My most noble lord and king,' said sir Lancelot, 'ye may say what ye will, for ye wot well with yourself I will not strive. But thereas ye say that I have slain your good knights, I wot well that I have done so, and that me sore repenteth; but I was forced to do battle with them in saving of my life, other else I must have suffered them to have slain me. And as for my lady queen Guenevere, except your person of your highness and my lord sir Gawain, there nis no knight under heaven that dare make it good upon me that ever I was traitor unto your person. And where it please you to say that I have holden my lady, your queen, years and winters, unto that I shall ever make a large answer, and prove it upon any knight that beareth the life, except your person and sir Gawain, that my lady, queen Guenevere, is as true a lady unto your person as is any lady living unto her lord, and that will I make good with my hands. Howbeit it hath liked her good grace to have me in favour and cherish me more than any other knight, and unto my power again I have deserved her love. For oftentimes, my lord, ye have consented that she should have be burnt and destroyed in your heat, and then it fortuned me to do battle for her, and or I departed from her adversary they confessed their untruth and she full worshipfully excused. And at such times, my lord Arthur,' said sir Lancelot, 'ye loved me and thanked me when I saved your queen from the fire, and then ye promised me for ever to be my good lord. And now methinketh ye reward me evil for my good service. And, my lord, meseemeth I had lost a great part of my worship in my knighthood and I had suffered my lady, your queen, to have been burnt, and insomuch as she should have been burnt for my sake; for sithen I have done battles for your queen in other quarrels than in mine own quarrel, meseemeth now I had more right to do battle for her in her right quarrel. And therefore, my good and gracious lord,' said sir Lancelot, 'take your queen unto your good grace, for she is both true and good.'

'Fie on thee, false recrayed knight!' said sir Gawain. 'For I let thee wit: my lord, mine uncle king Arthur shall have his queen and thee both maugre thy visage, and slay you both and save you whether it please him.'

'It may well be,' said sir Lancelot, 'but wit thou well, my lord sir Gawain, and me list to come out of this castle ye should win me and the queen more harder than ever ye won a strong battle.'

'Now, fie on thy proud words!' said sir Gawain. 'As for my lady the queen, wit thou well I will never say of her shame. But thou, false and recrayed knight,' said sir Gawain, 'what cause haddest thou to slay my good brother sir Gareth that loved thee more than me and all my kin? And alas, thou madest him knight, thine own hands! Why slewest thou him that loved thee so well?'

'For to excuse me,' said sir Lancelot, 'it boteneth me not, but by Jesu, and by the faith that I owe unto the high Order of Knighthood, I would with as good a will have slain my nephew, sir Bors de Ganis, at that time. And alas, that ever I was so unhappy,' said sir Lancelot, 'that I had not seen sir Gareth and sir Gaheris!'

'Thou liest, recrayed knight,' said sir Gawain. 'Thou slewest them in the despite of me. And therefore wit thou well, sir Lancelot, I shall make war upon thee, and all the while that I may live be thine enemy!'

'That me repents,' said sir Lancelot, 'for well I understand it boteneth me not to seek none accordment while ye, sir Gawain, are so mischievously set. And if ye were not, I would not doubt to have the good grace of my lord king Arthur.'

'I lieve well, false recrayed knight, for thou hast many long days overled me and us all, and destroyed many of our good knights.'

'Sir, ye say as it pleaseth you,' said sir Lancelot, 'yet may it never be said on me and openly proved that ever I by forecast of treason slew no good knight as ye, my lord sir Gawain, have done; and so did I never but in my defence, that I was driven thereto in saving of my life.'

'Ah! thou false knight,' said sir Gawain, 'that thou meanest by sir Lamorak. But wit thou well I slew him!'

'Sir, ye slew him not yourself,' said sir Lancelot, 'for it had been overmuch on hand for you to have slain him;* for he was one of the best knights christened of his age. And it was great pity of his death!'

'Well, well, sir Lancelot,' said sir Gawain, 'sithen thou enbraidest me of sir Lamorak, wit thou well, I shall never leave thee till I have thee at such avail that thou shalt not escape my hands.'

'I trust you well enough,' said sir Lancelot. 'And ye may get me, I get but little mercy.'

But the French book saith king Arthur would have taken his queen again and to have been accorded with sir Lancelot, but sir Gawain would not suffer him by no manner of mean. And so sir Gawain made many men to blow upon sir Lancelot, and so all at once they called him 'False recrayed knight.' But when sir Bors de Ganis, sir Ector de Maris and sir Lionel heard this outcry they called unto them sir Palomides, sir Saphir's brother,* and sir Lavain and sir Urry with many mo knights of their blood, and all they went unto sir Lancelot and said thus: 'My lord, wit you well we have great scorn of the great rebukes that we have heard sir Gawain say unto you. Wherefore we pray you, and charge you as ye will have our service, keep us no longer within these walls, for we let you wit plainly we will ride into the field and do battle with them. For ye fare as a man that were afeared, and for all your* fair speech it will not avail you, for wit you well sir Gawain will never suffer you to accord with king Arthur. And therefore fight for your life and right, and ye dare.' 'Alas,' said sir Lancelot, 'for to ride out of this castle and to do battle I am full loth.'

Then sir Lancelot spoke on height unto king Arthur and sir Gawain: 'My lord, I require and beseech you, sithen that I am thus required and conjured to ride into the field, that neither you, my lord king Arthur, nother you, sir Gawain, come not into the field.'

'What shall we do?' then said sir Gawain. 'Is not this the king's quarrel to fight with thee? And also it is my quarrel to fight with thee because of the death of my brother, sir Gareth.'

'Then must I needs unto battle,' said sir Lancelot. 'Now wit you well, my lord Arthur and sir Gawain, ye will repent it whensomever I do battle with you.' And so then they departed either from other.

And then either party made them ready on the morn for to do battle, and great purveyance was made on both sides. And sir Gawain let purvey many knights for to wait upon sir Lancelot for to overset him and to slay him. And on the morn at undern king Arthur was ready in the field with three great hosts. And then sir Lancelot's fellowship came out at the three gates in full good array. And sir Lionel came in the foremost battle, and sir Lancelot came in the middle, and sir Bors came out at the third gate. And thus they came in order and rule as full noble knights. And ever sir Lancelot charged all his knights in any wise to save king Arthur and sir Gawain.

Then came forth sir Gawain from the king's host and proffered to joust. And sir Lionel was a fierce knight, and lightly he encountered with him, and there sir Gawain smote sir Lionel throughout the body that he dashed to the earth like as he had been dead. And then sir Ector de Maris and other mo bore him into the castle.

And anon there began a great stour and much people were slain. And ever sir Lancelot did what he might to save the people on king Arthur's party. For sir Bors and sir Palomides and sir Saphir overthrew many knights, for they were deadly knights, and sir Blamour de Ganis and sir Bleoberis, with sir Bellinger le Bewse, these six knights did much harm. And ever was king Arthur about sir Lancelot to have slain him, and ever sir Lancelot suffered him and would not strike again. So sir Bors encountered with king Arthur, and sir Bors smote him, and so he alight and drew his sword and said to sir Lancelot, 'Sir, shall I make an end of this war?' (for he meant to have slain him). 'Not so hardy,' said sir Lancelot, 'upon pain of thy head, that thou touch him no more! For I will never see that most noble king that made me knight nother slain nor shamed.'

And therwithal sir Lancelot alight of his horse and took up the king and horsed him again, and said thus: 'My lord the king, for God's love, stint this strife, for ye get here no worship and I would do mine utterance. But always I forbear you, and ye nor none of yours forbeareth not me. And therefore, my lord, I pray you remember what I have done in many places, and now am I evil rewarded.'

So when king Arthur was on horseback he looked on sir Lancelot; then the tears burst out of his eyen, thinking of the great courtesy that was in sir Lancelot more than in any other man. And therewith the king rode his way and might no longer behold him, saying to himself, 'Alas, alas, that ever yet this war began!'

And then either party of the battles withdrew them to repose them, and buried the dead, and searched the wounded men and laid to their wounds soft salves. And thus they endured that night till on the morn.

And on the morn by undern they made them ready to do battle, and then sir Bors led the vanguard. So upon the morn there came sir Gawain, as brim as any boar, with a great spear in his hand. And when sir Bors saw him he thought to revenge his brother, sir Lionel, of the despite sir Gawain gave him the other day. And so, as they that knew either other, fewtred their spears, and with all their might of their horses and themself so fiercely they met togethers and so felonously that either bore other through, and so they fell both to the bare earth.

And then the battle joined, and there was much slaughter on both parties. Then sir Lancelot rescued sir Bors and sent him into the castle, but neither sir Gawain nother sir Bors died not of their wounds, for they were well holpen.

Then sir Lavain and sir Urry prayed sir Lancelot to do his pain and fight as they had done*—'For we see that ye forbear and spare and that doth us much harm. And therefore we pray you spare not your enemies no more than they do you.' 'Alas,' said sir Lancelot, 'I have no heart to fight against my lord Arthur, for ever meseemeth I do not as me ought to do.' 'My lord,' said sir Palomides, 'though ye spare them, never so much all this day they will can you thank; and if they may get you at avail, ye are but a dead man.'

So then sir Lancelot understood that they said him truth. Then he strained himself more than he did toforehand, and because* his nephew, sir Bors, was sore wounded he pained himself the more. And so within a little while, by evensong time, sir Lancelot's party the better stood, for their horses went in blood past the fetlocks, there were so many people slain. And then for very pity sir Lancelot withheld his knights and suffered king Arthur's party to withdraw them inside. And so he withdrew his meyny into the castle, and either parties buried the dead and put salve unto the wounded men. So when sir Gawain was hurt, they on king Arthur's party were not so orgulous as they were toforehand to do battle.

So of this war that was between king Arthur and sir Lancelot it was noised through all Christian realms, and so it came at the last by relation unto the Pope. And then the Pope took a consideration of the great goodness of king Arthur and of the high prowess of sir Lancelot, that was called the most noblest knight of the world. Wherefore the Pope called unto him a noble clerk that at that time was there present (the French book saith it was the Bishop of Rochester) and the Pope gave him bulls under lead, and sent them unto the king, charging him upon pain of interdicting of all England that he take his queen again and accord with sir Lancelot.

So when this Bishop was come unto Carlisle he showed the king his bulls, and when the king understood them he wist not what to do. But full fain he would have been accorded with sir Lancelot, but sir Gawain would not suffer him. But to have the queen he thereto agreed, but in no wise he would suffer the king to accord with sir Lancelot; but as for the queen, he consented. So the Bishop had of the king his great seal and his assurance, as he was a true and anointed king, that sir Lancelot should go safe and come safe, and that the queen should not be spoken* unto of the king, nother of none other, for nothing done of time past. And of all these appointments the Bishop brought with him sure assurance* and writing to show unto sir Lancelot.

E

So when the Bishop was come to Joyous Gard, there he showed sir Lancelot how he came from the Pope with writing unto king Arthur and unto him. And there he told him the perils, if he withheld the queen from the king. 'Sir, it was never in my thought,' said sir Lancelot, 'to withhold the queen from my lord Arthur, but I keep her for this cause, insomuch as she should have be burnt for my sake. Meseemed it was my part to save her life and put her from that danger till better recover might come. And now I thank God,' said sir Lancelot, 'that the Pope hath made her peace. For God knoweth,' said sir Lancelot, 'I will be a thousandfold more gladder to bring her again than ever I was of her taking away, with this I may be sure to come safe and go safe, and that the queen shall have her liberty as she had before, and never for nothing that hath be surmised afore this time that she never from this stand in no peril. For else,' said sir Lancelot, 'I dare adventure me to keep her from an harder shower than ever yet I had.'

'Sir, it shall not need you,' said the Bishop, 'to dread thus much, for wit you well, the Pope must be obeyed, and it were not the Pope's worship nother my poor honesty to know you distressed, nother the queen nother in peril nother shamed.' And then he showed sir Lancelot all his writing both from the Pope and king Arthur.

'This is sure enough,' said sir Lancelot, 'for full well I dare trust my lord's own writing and his seal, for he was never shamed of his promise. Therefore,' said sir Lancelot unto the Bishop, 'ye shall ride unto the king afore and recommend me unto his good grace, and let him have knowledging that the same day eight days, by the grace of God, I myself shall bring the queen unto him. And then say ye to my most redoubted king that I will say largely for the queen, that I shall none except, for dread nother for fear, but the king himself and my lord sir Gawain. And that is for the king's love more than for himself.'

So the Bishop departed and came to the king to Carlisle, and told him all how sir Lancelot answered him, so that made the tears fall out at the king's eyen. Then sir Lancelot purveyed him an hundred knights, and all well clothed in green velvet, and their horses trapped in the same to the heels. And every knight held a branch of olive in his hand in tokening of peace. And the queen had four-and-twenty gentlewomen following her in the same wise. And sir Lancelot had twelve coursers following him, and on every courser sat a young gentleman. And al they were arrayed in white velvet with sarps of gold about their quarters, and the horse trapped in the same wise down to the heels with many ouches, yset with stones and pearls in gold, to the number of a thousand. And in the same wise was the queen arrayed, and sir Lancelot in the same, of white cloth of gold tissue.

And right so as ye have heard, as the French book maketh mention, he rode with the queen from Joyous Gard to Carlisle. And so sir Lancelot rode throughout Carlisle, and so into the castle, that all men might behold them. And there was many a weeping eyen. And then sir Lancelot himself alight and voided his horse and took adown the queen, and so led her where king Arthur was in his seat. And sir Gawain sat afore him, and many other great lords.

So when sir Lancelot saw the king and sir Gawain, then he led the queen by the arm, and then he kneeled down and the queen both. Wit you well, then was there many a bold knight with king Arthur that wept as tenderly as they had seen all their kin dead afore them! So the king sat still and said no word. And when sir Lancelot saw his countenance he arose up and pulled up the queen with him, and thus he said full knightly:

'My most redoubted king, ye shall understand, by the Pope's commandment and yours I have brought to you my lady the queen, as right requireth. And if there be any knight, of what degree that ever he be of, except your person, that will say or dare say but that she is true and clean to you, I here, myself, sir Lancelot du Lake, will make it good upon his body that she is a true lady unto you.

'But, sir, liars ye have listened, and that hath caused great debate betwixt you and me. For time hath been, my lord Arthur, that ye were greatly pleased with me when I did battle for my lady, your queen; and full well ye know, my most noble king, that she hath be put to great wrong or this time. And sithen it pleased you at many times that I should fight for her, therefore meseemeth, my good lord, I had more cause to rescue her from the fire when she should have been burnt for my sake.

'For they that told you tho tales were liars, and so it fell upon them: for by likelihood, had not the might of God been with me, I might never have endured with fourteen knights. And they were armed and afore purposed, and I unarmed and not purposed; for I was sent unto my lady, your queen, I wot not for what cause. But I was not so soon within the chamber door but anon sir Agravain and sir Mordred called me traitor and false recrayed knight.'

'By my faith, they called thee right!' said sir Gawain.

'My lord, sir Gawain,' said sir Lancelot, 'in their quarrel they proved not themself the best, nother in the right.'

'Well, well, sir Lancelot,' said the king, 'I have given you no cause to do to me as ye have done, for I have worshipped you and yours more than any other knights.'

'My good* lord,' said sir Lancelot, 'so ye be not displeased, ye shall understand that I and mine have done you oftentimes better service than any other knights have done in many divers places. And where ye have been full hard bestead divers times, I have rescued you from many dangers, and ever unto my power I was glad to please you and my lord sir Gawain. In jousts and in tournaments and in battles set, both on horseback and on foot, I have often rescued you, and you, my lord sir Gawain, and many mo of your knights in many divers places.

'For now I will make avaunt,' said sir Lancelot, 'I will that ye all wit that as yet I found never no manner of knight but that I was over hard for him and I had done mine utterance, God graunt mercy! Howbeit I have be matched with good knights, as sir Tristram and sir Lamorak, but ever I had favour unto them and a deeming what they were. And I take God to record, I never was wroth nor greatly heavy with no good knight and I saw him busy and about to win worship; and glad I was ever when I found a good knight that might anything endure me on horseback and on foot. Howbeit sir Carados of the Dolorous Tower was a full noble knight and a passing strong man, and that wot ye, my lord sir Gawain; for he might well be called a noble knight when he by fine force pulled you out of your saddle and bound you overthwart afore him to his saddle-bow. And there, my lord sir Gawain, I rescued you and slew him afore your sight. Also I found your brother sir Gaheris, and sir Tarquin leading him bounden afore him; and there also I rescued your brother and slew sir Tarquin and delivered three score and four of my lord Arthur's knights out of his prison. And now I dare say,' said sir Lancelot, 'I met never with so strong a knight nor so well-fighting as was sir Carados and sir Tarquin, for they and I fought to the uttermost.

'And therefore,' said sir Lancelot unto sir Gawain, 'meseemeth ye

ought of right to remember this; for, and I might have your good
will, I would trust to God for to have my lord Arthur's good
grace.'

'Sir, the king may do as he will,' said sir Gawain, 'but wit thou
well, sir Lancelot, thou and I shall never be accorded while we live,
for thou hast slain three of my brethren. And two of them thou slew
traitorly and piteously, for they bore none harness against thee, nother
none would do.'

'Sir, God would they had been armed,' said sir Lancelot, 'for then
had they been on live. And wit you well, sir Gawain, as for Gareth,
I loved no kinsman I had more than I loved him, and ever while I
live,' said sir Lancelot, 'I will bewail sir Gareth his death, not all only
for the great fear I have of you, but for many causes which causeth
me to be sorrowful. One is that I made him knight; another is, I wot
well he loved me aboven all other knights; and the third is, he was
passing noble and true, courteous and gentle and well-conditioned.
The fourth is, I wist well, anon as I heard that sir Gareth was dead, I
knew well that I should never after have your love, my lord sir Gawain,
but everlasting war betwixt us. And also I wist well that ye would
cause my noble lord king Arthur for ever to be my mortal foe. And as
Jesu be my help, and by my knighthood, I slew never sir Gareth nother
his brother by my willing, but alas that ever they were unarmed that
unhappy day!

'But this much I shall offer me to you,' said sir Lancelot, 'if it may
please the king's good grace and you, my lord sir Gawain: I shall first
begin at Sandwich, and there I shall go in my shirt, bare-foot. And at
every ten miles end I shall found and gar make an house of religious,*
of what order that ye will assign me, with an holy convent, to sing
and read day and night in especial for sir Gareth sake and sir Gaheris.
And this shall I perform from Sandwich unto Carlisle. And every
house shall have sufficient livelihood. And this shall I perform while
that I have any livelihood in Christendom. And there is none of all
these religious places but they shall be performed, furnished and
garnished with all things as an holy place ought to be, I promise you
faithfully.* And this, sir Gawain, me thinketh* were fairer and more
holier and more perfect to their souls than ye, my most noble king,
and you, sir Gawain, to war upon me, for thereby shall ye get none
avail.'

Then all the knights and ladies that were there wept as they were mad, and the tears fell on king Arthur his cheeks.

'Sir Lancelot,' said sir Gawain, 'I have right well heard thy language and thy great proffers. But wit thou well, let the king do as it pleaseth him, I will never forgive thee my brothers' death, and in especial the death of my brother sir Gareth. And if mine uncle, king Arthur, will accord with thee, he shall lose my service, for wit thou well,' said sir Gawain, 'thou art both false to the king and to me.'

'Sir,' said sir Lancelot, 'he beareth not the life that may make it good! And ye, sir Gawain, will charge me with so high a thing, ye must pardon me, for then needs must I answer you.'

'Nay, nay,' said sir Gawain, 'we are past that as at this time, and that causeth the Pope, for he hath charged mine uncle the king that he shall take again his queen and to accord with thee, sir Lancelot, as for this season, and therefore thou shalt go safe as thou come. But in this land thou shalt not abide past a fifteen days, such summons I give thee, for so the king and we were condescended and accorded or thou came. And else,' said sir Gawain, 'wit thou well, thou should not a comen here but if it were magré thine head. And if it were not for the Pope's commandment,' said sir Gawain, 'I should do battle with thee mine own hands, body for body, and prove it upon thee that thou hast been both false unto mine uncle, king Arthur, and to me both; and that shall I prove on thy body, when thou art departed from hence, wheresomever that I find thee!'

Then sir Lancelot sighed, and therewith the tears fell on his cheeks, and then he said thus:

'Most noblest Christian realm, whom I have loved aboven all other realms! And in thee I have gotten a great part of my worship, and now that I shall depart in this wise, truly me repents that ever I came in this realm, that I should be thus shamefully banished, undeserved and causeless! But fortune is so variant, and the wheel so mutable, that there is no constant abiding. And that may be proved by many old chronicles, as of noble Hector of Troy and Alexander the mighty conqueror, and many mo other: when they were most in their royalty, they alight passing low. And so fareth it by me,' said sir Lancelot, 'for in this realm I had worship, and by me and mine all the whole Round Table hath been increased more in worship, by me and mine, than ever it was by any of you all.

'And therefore wit thou well, sir Gawain, I may live upon my lands as well as any knight that here is. And if ye, my most redoubted king, will come upon my lands with sir Gawain to war upon me, I must endure you as well as I may. But as to you, sir Gawain, if that ye come there, I pray you charge me not with treason nother felony, for and ye do, I must answer you.'

'Do thou thy best,' said sir Gawain, 'and therefore hie thee fast that thou were gone! And wit thou well we shall soon come after and break the strongest castle that thou hast, upon thy head!'

'It shall not need that,' said sir Lancelot, 'for and I were as orgulous set as ye are, wit you well I should meet you in mids of the field.'

'Make thou no more language,' said sir Gawain, 'but deliver the queen from thee, and pick thee lightly out of this court!'

'Well,' said sir Lancelot, 'and I had wist of this shortcoming, I would a advised me twice or that I had come here. For and the queen had be so dear unto me as ye noise her, I durst have kept her from the fellowship of the best knights under heaven.'

And then sir Lancelot said unto queen Guenevere in hearing of the king and them all, 'Madam, now I must depart from you and this noble fellowship for ever. And sithen it is so, I beseech you to pray for me, and I shall pray for you. And tell ye me and if ye be hard bestead by any false tongues. But lightly, my good lady, send me word. And if any knight's hands under the heaven may deliver you by battle, I shall deliver you.'

And therewithal sir Lancelot kissed the queen, and then he said all openly, 'Now let see whatsomever he be in this place that dare say the queen is not true unto my lord Arthur. Let see who will speak, and he dare speak.'

And therewith he brought the queen to the king, and then sir Lancelot took his leave and departed. And there nother king, duke, earl, baron, nor knight, lady nor gentlewoman, but all they wept as people out of their* mind, except sir Gawain. And when this noble knight sir Lancelot took his horse to ride out of Carlisle, there was sobbing and weeping for pure dole of his departing.

And so he took his way to Joyous Gard, and then ever after he called it the 'Dolorous Gard.' And thus departed sir Lancelot from the court for ever.

And so when he came to Joyous Gard he called his fellowship unto him and asked them what they would do. Then they answered all wholly togethers with one voice, they would do as he would do.

'Then, my fair fellows,' said sir Lancelot, 'I must depart out of this noble realm. And now I shall depart, it grieveth me sore, for I shall depart with no worship; for a flemed man departeth never out of a realm with no worship. And that is to me great heaviness, for ever I fear after my days that men shall chronicle upon me that I was flemed out of this land. And else, my fair lords, be ye sure, and I had not dread shame, my lady queen Guenevere and I should never have departed.'

Then spoke noble knights, as sir Palomides and sir Saphir, his brother, and sir Bellinger le Bewse, and sir Urry with sir Lavain, with many other: 'Sir, and ye will so be disposed to abide in this land we will never fail you. And if ye list not abide in this land, there is none of the good knights that here be that will fail you, for many causes. One is, all we that be not of your blood shall never be welcome unto the court. And sithen it liked us to take a part with you in your distress in this realm, wit you well, it shall like us as well to go in other countries with you and there to take such part as ye do.'

'My fair lords,' said sir Lancelot, 'I well understand you, and as I can, I thank you. And ye shall understand, such livelihood as I am born unto I shall depart with you in this manner of wise: that is for to say, I shall depart all my livelihood and all my lands freely among you, and myself will have as little as any of you; for, have I sufficient that may long unto my person, I will ask none other riches nother array. And I trust to God to maintain you on my lands as well as ever ye were maintained.'

Then spake all the knights at once: 'Have he shame that will leave you! For we all understand, in this realm will be no quiet but ever debate and strife, now the fellowship of the Round Table is broken. For by the noble fellowship of the Round Table was king Arthur upborne, and by their noblesse the king and all the realm was ever in quiet and rest. And a great part,' they said all, 'was because of your most noblesse, sir Lancelot.'

'Now, truly I thank you all of your good saying! Howbeit I wot well that in me was not all the stability of this realm, but in that I might I did my devoir. And well I am sure I knew many rebellions in my days that by me and mine were peaced. And that I trow we all shall hear of in short space, and that me sore repenteth. For ever I dread me,' said sir Lancelot, 'that sir Mordred will make trouble, for he is passing envious and applieth him much to trouble.'

And so they were accorded to depart with sir Lancelot to his lands. And to make short this tale, they trussed and payed all that would ask them; and wholly an hundred knights departed with sir Lancelot at once, and made their avows they would never leave him for weal ne for woe.

And so they shipped at Cardiff, and sailed unto Benwick. Some men call it Bayonne and some men call it Beaune, where the wine of Beaune is. But say the sooth, sir Lancelot and his nephews was lord of all France and of all the lands that belonged unto France. He and his kindred rejoiced it all through sir Lancelot's noble prowess.

And then he stuffed and furnished and garnished all his noble towns and castles. Then all the people of tho lands came unto sir Lancelot on foot and hands. And so when he had stablished all those countries, he shortly called a parliament; and there he crowned sir Lionel king of France, and sir Bors he crowned him king of all king Claudas lands, and sir Ector de Maris, sir Lancelot's younger brother, he crowned him king of Benwick and king of all Guienne, which was sir Lancelot's own lands. And he made sir Ector prince of them all.

And thus he departed his lands and advanced all his noble knights. And first he advanced them of his blood, as sir Blamour, he made him duke of Limousine in Guienne, and sir Bleoberis, he made him duke of Poitiers. And sir Gahalantin, he made him duke of Auvergne; and sir Galihodin, he made him duke of Sentonge; and sir Galihud, he made him earl of Perigot; and sir Menaduke, he made him earl of Roerge; and sir Villiers the Valiant, he made him earl of Bearn; and sir Hebes le Renownes, he made him earl of Comange; and sir Lavain, he made him earl of Armignac; and sir Urry, he made him earl of Estrake; and sir Neroveus, he made him earl of Pardiak; and sir Plenorius, he made him earl of Foise; and sir Selises of the Dolorous Tower, he made him earl of Marsac; and sir Melias de le Ile, he made him earl of Tursanke; and sir Bellinger le Bewse, he made him earl of the Landes; and sir Palomides, he made him duke of Provence; and sir Saphir, he made him duke of Languedoc. And sir Clegis, he gave him the earldom of Argente; and sir Sadok, he gave him the earldom of Sarlat; and sir Dinas le Seneschal, he made him duke of Anjou; and sir Clarrus, he made him duke of Normandy.

Thus sir Lancelot rewarded his noble knights, and many mo that meseemeth it were too long to rehearse.

3. The Siege of Benwick

(Caxton XX, 19–22)

So leave we sir Lancelot in his lands and his noble knights with him, and return we again unto king Arthur and unto sir Gawain, that made a great host aready to the number of three score thousand. And all thing was made ready for shipping to pass over the sea, to war upon sir Lancelot and upon his lands. And so they shipped at Cardiff.

And there king Arthur made sir Mordred chief ruler of all England, and also he put the queen under his governance. Because sir Mordred was king Arthur's son he gave him the rule of his land and of his wife.

And so the king passed the sea and landed upon sir Lancelot's lands, and there he burnt and wasted, through the vengeance of sir Gawain, all that they might overrun.

So when this word was come unto sir Lancelot, that king Arthur and sir Gawain were landed upon his lands and made full great destruction and waste, then spoke sir Bors and said, 'My lord, sir Lancelot, it is shame that we suffer them thus to ride over our lands. For wit you well, suffer ye them as long as ye will, they will do you no favour and they may handle you.'

Then said sir Lionel, that was ware and wise, 'My lord, sir Lancelot, I will give you this counsel: let us keep our strongwalled towns until they have hunger and cold, and blow on their nails; and then let us freshly set upon them and shred them down as sheep in a fold, that ever after aliens may take example how they land upon our lands!'

Then spoke king Bagdemagus to sir Lancelot and said, 'Sir, your courtesy will shend us all, and your courtesy hath waked all this sorrow; for and they thus override our lands, they shall by process bring us all to nought while we thus in holes us hide.'

Then said sir Galihud unto sir Lancelot, 'Sir, here been knights come of king's blood that will not long droop and dare within these walls. Therefore give us leave, like as we been knights, to meet them in the field, and we shall slay them and so deal with them that they shall curse the time that ever they came into this country.'

Then spoke seven brethren of North Wales which were seven noble knights; for a man might seek seven kings' lands or he might find such seven knights. And these seven noble knights said all at once, 'Sir Lancelot, for Christ's sake, let us ride out with sir Galihud, for we were never wont to cower in castles nother in noble towns.'

Then spoke sir Lancelot, that was master and governor of them all, and said, 'My fair lords, wit you well I am full loth to ride out with my knights for shedding of Christian blood; and yet my lands I understand be full bare for to sustain any host awhile, for the mighty wars that whilom made king Claudas upon this country and upon my father, king Ban, and on mine uncle, king Bors. Howbeit we will as at this time keep our strong walls. And I shall send a messenger unto my lord Arthur a treatise for to take, for better is peace than always war'.

So sir Lancelot sent forth a damsel with a dwarf with her, requiring king Arthur to leave his warring upon his lands. And so she* start upon a palfrey, and the* dwarf ran by her side, and when she came to the pavilion of king Arthur, there she alight. And there met her a gentle knight, sir Lucan the Butler, and said, 'Fair damsel, come ye from sir Lancelot du Lake?'

'Yea, sir,' she said, 'therefore came I hither to speak with my lord the king.'

'Alas,' said sir Lucan, 'my lord Arthur would accord with sir Lancelot, but sir Gawain will not suffer him.' And then he said, 'I pray to God, damsel, that ye may speed well, for all we that been about the king would that Lancelot did best of any knight living.' And so with this sir Lucan led the damsel to the king, where he sat with sir Gawain, for to hear what she would say. So when she had told her tale the water ran out of the king's eyen. And all the lords were full glad for to advise the king to be accorded with sir Lancelot, save all only sir Gawain. And he said, 'My lord, mine uncle, what will ye do? Will ye now turn again, now ye are passed this far upon your journey? All the world will speak of you villainy and shame.'

'Now,' said king Arthur, 'wit you well, sir Gawain, I will do as ye advise me; and yet meseemeth,' said king Arthur, 'his fair proffers were not good to be refused. But sithen I am come so far upon this jnorney, I will that ye give the damsel her answer, for I may not speak to her for pity; for her proffers been so large.'

Then sir Gawain said unto the damsel thus: 'Say ye to sir Lancelot that it is waste labour now to sue to mine uncle. For tell him, and he would have made any labour for peace, he should have made it or this time, for tell him now it is too late. And say to him that I, sir Gawain, so send him word, that I promise him by the faith that I owe to God and to knighthood, I shall never leave him till he hath slain me or I him!' So the damsel wept and departed, and so there was many a weeping eye. And then sir Lucan brought the damsel to her palfrey.

And so she came to sir Lancelot, where he was among all his knights, and when sir Lancelot had heard her answer, then the tears ran down by his cheeks. And then his noble knights strode about him and said, 'Sir Lancelot, wherefore make ye such cheer? Now think what ye are, and what men we are, and let us, noble knights, match them in mids of the field.'

'That may be lightly done,' said sir Lancelot. 'But I was never so loth to do battle. And therefore I pray you, sirs, as ye love me, be ruled at this time as I will have you. For I will always flee that noble king that made me knight; and when I may no farther, I must needs defend me. And that will be more worship for me and us all than to compare with that noble king whom we have all served.'

Then they held their language, and as that night they took their rest. And upon the morning early, in the dawning of the day, as knights looked out they saw the city of Benwick besieged round about, and gan fast to set up ladders. And they within kept them out of the town and beat them mightily from the walls.

Then came forth sir Gawain, well armed, upon a stiff steed, and he came before the chief gate with his spear in his hand, crying: 'Where art thou, sir Lancelot? Is there none of all your proud knights that dare break a spear with me?'

Then sir Bors made him ready and came forth out of the town. And there sir Gawain encountered with sir Bors, and at that time he smote him down from his horse, and almost he had slain him. And so sir Bors was rescued and borne into the town.

Then came forth sir Lionel, brother to sir Bors, and thought to revenge him; and either fewtred their spears and so ran togethers. And there they met spiteously, but sir Gawain had such a grace that he smote sir Lionel down, and wounded him there passingly sore. And then sir Lionel was rescued and borne into the town.

And thus sir Gawain came every day, and failed not but that he smote down one knight or other. So thus they endured half a year, and much slaughter was of people on both parties.

Then it befell upon a day that sir Gawain came afore the gates, armed at all pieces, on a noble horse, with a great spear in his hand, and then he cried with a loud voice and said,

'Where art thou now, thou false traitor, sir Lancelot? Why hidest* thou thyself within holes and walls like a coward? Look out, thou false traitor knight, and here I shall revenge upon thy body the death of my three brethren!'

And all this language heard sir Lancelot every deal. Then his kin and his knights drew about him, and all they said at once unto sir Lancelot, 'Sir, now must you defend you like a knight, other else ye be shamed for ever, for now ye be called upon treason, it is time for you to stir! For ye have slept overlong, and suffered overmuch.'

'So God me help,' said sir Lancelot, 'I am right heavy at sir Gawain's words, for now he chargeth me with a great charge. And therefore I wot as well as ye I must needs defend me, other else to be recreant.'

Then sir Lancelot bade saddle his strongest horse and bade let fetch his arms and bring all to the tower of the gate. And then sir Lancelot spoke on height unto the king and said,

'My lord Arthur, and noble king that made me knight! Wit you well I am right heavy for your sake and that ye thus sue upon me. And always I forbear you, for and I would be vengeable I might have met you in mids the field or this time, and there to have made your boldest knights full tame. And now I have forborne you and suffered you half a year, and sir Gawain, to do what ye would do. And now I may no longer suffer to endure, but needs I must defend myself, insomuch as sir Gawain hath becalled me of treason; which is greatly against my will that ever I should fight against any of your blood, but now I may not forsake it: for I am driven thereto as beast till a bay.'

Then sir Gawain said unto sir Lancelot, 'And thou durst do battle, leave thy babbling and come off, and let us ease our hearts!'

Then sir Lancelot armed him lightly* and mounted upon his horse, and either of them got great spears in their hands. And so the host without stood still all apart, and the noble knights of the city came a great number, that when king Arthur saw the number of men and knights he marvelled and said to himself, 'Alas, that ever sir Lancelot was against me! For now I see that he hath forborne me.'

And so the covenant was made, there should no man nigh them nother deal with them till the tone were dead other yolden.

Then sir Lancelot and sir Gawain departed a great way in sunder, and then they came togethers with all their horse mights as fast as they might run, and either smote other in mids of their shields. But the knights were so strong and their spears so big that their horses might not endure their buffets, and so their horses fell to the earth. And then they avoided their horses and dressed their shields afore them. Then they stood togethers and gave many sad strokes on diverse places of their bodies, that the blood burst out on many sides.

Then had sir Gawain such a grace and gift that an holy man had given him, that every day in the year, from undern till high noon, his might increased tho three hours as much as thrice his strength. And that caused sir Gawain to win great honour. And for his sake king Arthur made an ordinance that all manner of battles for any quarrels that should be done afore king Arthur should begin at undern; and all was done for sir Gawain's love, that by likelihood if sir Gawain were on the tone party, he should have the better in battle while his strength endured three hours. But there were that time but few knights living that knew this advantage that sir Gawain had, but king Arthur all only.

So sir Lancelot fought with sir Gawain, and when sir Lancelot felt his might evermore increase, sir Lancelot wondered and dread him sore to be shamed; for, as the French book saith, he weened, when he felt sir Gawain* double his strength, that he had been a fiend and none earthly man. Wherefore sir Lancelot traced and traversed, and covered himself with his shield, and kept his might and his breath during three hours. And that while sir Gawain gave him many sad brunts and many sad strokes that all knights that beheld sir Lancelot marvelled how he might endure him, but full little understood they that travail that sir Lancelot had to endure him.

And then when it was past noon sir Gawain's strength was gone and he had no more but his own might. When sir Lancelot felt him so come down, then he stretched him up and strode near sir Gawain and said thus: 'Now I feel ye have done your worst! And now my lord sir Gawain, I must do my part, for many a great and grievous strokes I have endured you this day with great pain.'

And so sir Lancelot doubled his strokes and gave sir Gawain such a stroke upon the helmet that sideling he fell down upon his one side. And sir Lancelot withdrew him from him.

'Why withdrawest thou thee?' said sir Gawain. 'Turn again, false traitor knight, and slay me out! For and thou leave me thus, anon as I am whole I shall do battle with thee again.'

'Sir,' said sir Lancelot, 'I shall endure you, by God's grace! But wit thou well, sir Gawain, I will never smite a felled knight.'

And so sir Lancelot departed and went unto the city. (And sir Gawain was borne unto king Arthur's pavilion, and anon leeches were brought unto him of the best, and searched and salved him with soft ointments.) And then sir Lancelot said, 'Now have good day, my lord the king! For wit you well ye win no worship at these walls, for and I would my knights outbring, there should many a doughty man die. And therefore, my lord Arthur, remember you of old kindness, and howsomever I fare, Jesu be your guide in all places.'

'Now, alas,' said the king, 'that ever this unhappy war began! For ever sir Lancelot forbeareth me in all places, and in like wise my kin, and that is seen well this day, what courtesy he showed my nephew, sir Gawain.'

Then king Arthur fell sick for sorrow of sir Gawain, that he was so sore hurt, and because of the war betwixt him and sir Lancelot. So after that they on king Arthur's party kept the siege with little war withoutforth, and they withinforth kept their walls and defended them when need was.

Thus sir Gawain lay sick and unsound three weeks in his tents with all manner of leechcraft that might be had. And as soon as sir Gawain might go and ride, he armed him at all points and bestrode a stiff courser and got a great spear in his hand, and so he came riding afore the chief gate of Benwick. And there he cried on height and said, 'Where art thou, sir Lancelot? Come forth, thou false traitor knight and recrayed, for I am here, sir Gawain, that will prove this that I say upon thee!'

And all this language sir Lancelot heard and said thus: 'Sir Gawain, me repents of your foul saying, that ye will not cease your language. For ye wot well, sir Gawain, I know your might and all that ye may do, and well ye wot, sir Gawain, ye may not greatly hurt me.'

'Come down, traitor knight,' said he, 'and make it good the contrary with thy hands! For it mis-happed me the last battle to be hurt of thy hands. Therefore, wit thou well, I am come this day to make amends, for I ween this day to lay thee as low as thou laidest me.'

'Jesu defend me,' said sir Lancelot, 'that ever I be so far in your danger as ye have been in mine, for then my days were done. But, sir* Gawain,' said sir Lancelot, 'ye shall not think that I shall tarry long, but sithen that ye unknightly call me thus of treason, ye shall have both your hands full of me.' And then sir Lancelot armed him at all points and mounted upon his horse and got a great spear in his hand and rode out at the gate. And both their hosts were assembled, of them without and within, and stood in array full manly, and both parties were charged to hold them still to see and behold the battle of these two noble knights.

And then they laid their spears in their rests and so came together as thunder. And sir Gawain broke his spear upon sir Lancelot in an hundred pieces unto* his hand, and sir Lancelot smote him with a greater might, that sir Gawain's horse feet raised, and so the horse and he fell to the earth. Then sir Gawain deliverly devoided his horse and put his shield afore him, and eagerly drew his sword and bade sir Lancelot, 'alight, traitor knight!' and said, 'If a mare's son hath failed me, wit thou well a king's son and a queen's son shall not fail thee!'

Then sir Lancelot devoided his horse and dressed his shield afore him and drew his sword, and so stood eagerly togethers and gave many sad strokes, that all men on both parties had thereof passing great* wonder.

But when sir Lancelot felt sir Gawain's might so marvellously increase, he then withheld his courage and his wind, and so he kept him under covert of his might and of his shield. He traced and traversed here and there, to break sir Gawain's strokes and his courage. And ever sir Gawain enforced himself with all his might and power to destroy sir Lancelot, for, as the French book saith, ever as sir Gawain's might increased, right so increased his wind and his evil will.

And thus he did great pain unto sir Lancelot three hours, that he had much ado to defend him. And when the three hours were passed, that he felt sir Gawain was come home to his own proper strength, then sir Lancelot said, 'Sir, now I have proved you twice that ye are a full dangerous knight and a wonderful man of your might! And many wonder deeds have ye done in your days, for by your might increasing ye have deceived many a full noble knight. And now I feel that ye have done your mighty deeds, now, wit you well, I must do my deeds!'

And then sir Lancelot strode near sir Gawain and doubled his strokes. And ever sir Gawain defended him mightily, but nevertheless sir Lancelot smote such a stroke upon his helm and upon the old wound that sir Gawain sank down and swooned. And anon as he did awake he waved and foined at sir Lancelot as he lay, and said, 'Traitor knight wit thou well I am not yet slain. Therefore come thou near me and perform this battle to the utterance!'

'I will no more do than I have done,' said sir Lancelot. 'For when I see you on foot I will do battle upon you all the while I see you stand upon your feet; but to smite a wounded man that may not stand, God defend me from such a shame!'

And then he turned him and went his way toward the city, and sir Gawain evermore calling him 'traitor knight' and said, 'Traitor knight! Wit thou well, sir Lancelot, when I am whole I shall do battle with thee* again, for I shall never leave thee till the tone of us be slain!'

Thus as this siege endured and as sir Gawain lay sick nearhand a month, and when he was well recovered and ready within three days to do battle again with sir Lancelot, right so came tidings unto king Arthur from England that made king Arthur and all his host to remove.

4. The Day of Destiny

(Caxton XXI, 1–7)

As sir Mordred was ruler of all England, he let make letters as though that they had come from beyond the sea, and the letters specified that king Arthur was slain in battle with sir Lancelot. Wherefore sir Mordred made a parliament, and called the lords together, and there he made them to choose him king. And so was he crowned at Canterbury, and held a feast there fifteen days.

And afterward he drew him unto Winchester, and there he took queen Guenevere, and said plainly that he would wed her (which was his uncle's wife and his father's wife). And so he made ready for the feast, and a day prefixed that they should be wedded; wherefore queen Guenevere was passing heavy. But she durst not discover her heart, but spoke fair, and agreed to sir Mordred's will.

F

And anon she desired of sir Mordred to go to London to buy all manner things that longed to the bridal. And because of her fair speech sir Mordred trusted her and gave her leave. And so when she came to London she took the Tower of London, and suddenly in all haste possible she stuffed it with all manner of victual, and well garnished it with men, and so kept it.

And when sir Mordred wist how he was beguiled* he was passing wroth out of measure. And short tale to make, he laid a mighty siege about the Tower, and made many assaults, and threw engines unto them, and shot great guns. But all might not prevail, for queen Guenevere would never, for fair speech nother for foul, never to trust unto sir Mordred to come in his hands again.

Then came the Bishop of Canterbury, which was a noble clerk and an holy man, and thus he said unto sir Mordred: 'Sir, what will ye do? Will ye first displease God and sithen shame yourself and all knighthood? For is not king Arthur your uncle, and no farther but your mother's brother, and upon her he himself begat you, upon his own sister? Therefore how may ye wed your own father's wife? And therefore, sir,' said the Bishop, 'leave this opinion, other else I shall curse you with book, bell and candle.'

'Do thou thy worst,' said sir Mordred, 'and I defy thee!'

'Sir,' said the Bishop, 'wit you well I shall not fear me to do that me ought to do. And also ye noise that my lord Arthur is slain, and that is not so, and therefore ye will make a foul work in this land!'

'Peace, thou false priest!' said sir Mordred, 'for and thou chafe me any more, I shall strike off thy head!'

So the Bishop departed, and did the cursing in the most orgulust wise that might be done. And then sir Mordred sought the Bishop of Canterbury for to have slain him. Then the Bishop fled, and took part of his good with him, and went nigh unto Glastonbury. And there he was a priest-hermit in a chapel, and lived in poverty and in holy prayers; for well he understood that mischievous war was at hand.

Then sir Mordred sought upon queen Guenevere by letters and sands, and by fair means and foul means, to have her to come out of the Tower of London. But all this availed nought, for she answered him shortly, openly and privily, that she had liefer slay herself than to be married with him.

Then came there word unto sir Mordred that king Arthur had

araised the siege from sir Lancelot and was coming homeward with a great host to be avenged upon sir Mordred; wherefore sir Mordred made write* writs unto all the barony of this land. And much people drew unto him; for then was the common voice among them that with king Arthur was never other life but war and strife, and with sir Mordred was great joy and bliss. Thus was king Arthur depraved, and evil said of; and many there were that king Arthur had brought up of nought, and given them lands, that might not then say him a good word.

Lo, ye all Englishmen, see ye not what a mischief here was? For he that was the most king and noblest knight of the world, and most loved the fellowship of noble knights, and by him they all were upholden, and yet might not these Englishmen hold them content with him. Lo thus was the old custom and usages of this land, and men say that we of this land have not yet lost that custom. Alas! this is a great default of us Englishmen, for there may no thing us please no term.

And so fared the people at that time; they were better pleased with sir Mordred than they were with the noble king Arthur, and much people drew unto sir Mordred and said they would abide with him for better and for worse. And so sir Mordred drew with a great host to Dover, for there he heard say that king Arthur would arrive, and so he thought to beat his own father from his own lands. And the most party of all England held with sir Mordred, for the people were so new-fangle.

And so as sir Mordred was at Dover with his host, so came king Arthur with a great navy of ships and galleys and carracks, and there was sir Mordred ready awaiting upon his landing, to let his own father to land upon the land that he was king over.

Then there was launching of great boats and small, and full of noble men of arms. And there was much slaughter of gentle knights, and many a full bold baron was laid full low on both parties. But king Arthur was so courageous that there might no manner of knight let him to land, and his knights fiercely followed him. And so they landed maugre sir Mordred's head and all his power, and put sir Mordred aback, that he fled and all his people.

So when this battle was done, king Arthur let search his people that were hurt and dead. And then was noble sir Gawain found in a great boat lying more than half dead. When king Arthur knew that he was laid so low he went unto him and so found him. And there the king made great sorrow out of measure, and took sir Gawain in his arms, and thrice he there swooned. And then when he was waked, king Arthur said,

'Alas! sir Gawain, my sister son, here now thou liest, the man in the world that I loved most. And now is my joy gone! For now, my nephew, sir Gawain, I will discover me unto you, that in your person and in sir Lancelot I most had my joy and mine affiance. And now have I lost my joy of you both, wherefore all mine earthly joy is gone from me!'

'Ah, mine uncle,' said sir Gawain, 'now I will that ye wit that my death-days be come! And all, I may wite mine own hastiness and my wilfulness, for through my wilfulness I was causer of mine own death. For I was this day hurt and smitten upon mine old wound that sir Lancelot gave me, and I feel myself that I must needs be dead by the hour of noon. And through me and my pride ye have all this shame and disease, for had that noble knight, sir Lancelot, been with you, as he was and would have been, this unhappy war had never been begun; for he, through his noble knighthood and his noble blood, held all your cankered enemies in subjection and danger. And now,' said sir Gawain, 'ye shall miss sir Lancelot. But alas that I would not accord with him! And therefore, fair uncle, I pray you that I may have paper, pen and ink, that I may write unto sir Lancelot a letter written with mine own hand.'

So, when paper, pen and ink was brought, then sir Gawain was set up weakly by king Arthur, for he was shriven a little afore. And then he took his pen and wrote thus, as the French book maketh mention:

'Unto thee, sir Lancelot, flower of all noble knights that ever I heard of or saw by my days, I, sir Gawain, king Lot's son of Orkney, and sister's son unto the noble king Arthur, send thee greeting, letting thee to have knowledge that the tenth day of May I was smitten upon the old wound that thou gave me afore the city of Benwick. And through that wound I am come to my death-day. And I will that all the world wit that I, sir Gawain, knight of the Table Round, sought my death, and not through thy deserving, but mine own seeking. Where-for I beseech thee, sir Lancelot, to return again unto this realm and see my tomb, and pray some prayer more other less for my soul. And this same day that I wrote the same schedule I was hurt to the death, which wound was first given of thine hand, sir Lancelot; for of a more nobler man might I not be slain.

'Also, sir Lancelot, for all the love that ever was betwixt us, make no tarrying, but come over the sea in all the goodly haste that ye may, with your noble knights, and rescue that noble king that made thee knight, for he is full straitly bestead with an false traitor which is my half-brother, sir Mordred. For he hath crowned himself king, and would have wedded my lady, queen Guenevere; and so had he done, had she not kept the Tower of London with strong hand. And so the tenth day of May last past my lord king Arthur and we all landed upon them at Dover, and there he put that false traitor, sir Mordred, to flight. And so it there misfortuned me to be smitten upon the stroke that ye gave me of old.

'And the date of this letter was written but two hours and an half afore my death, written with mine own hand and subscribed with part of my heart blood. And therefore I require thee, most famous knight of the world, that thou wilt see my tomb.'

And then he wept and king Arthur both, and swooned. And when they were awaked both, the king made sir Gawain to receive his sacrament, and then sir Gawain prayed the king for to send for sir Lancelot and to cherish him aboven all other knights.

And so at the hour of noon sir Gawain yielded up the ghost. And then the king let inter him in a chapel within Dover castle. And there yet all men may see the skull of him, and the same wound is seen that sir Lancelot gave in battle.

Then was it told the king that sir Mordred had pight a new field upon Barham Down. And so upon the morn king Arthur rode thither to him, and there was a great battle betwixt them, and much people were slain on both parties. But at the last king Arthur's party stood best, and sir Mordred and his party fled unto Canterbury.

And then the king let search all the downs for his knights that were slain and interred them. And salved them with soft salves that full sore were wounded. Then much people drew unto king Arthur, and then they said that sir Mordred warred upon king Arthur with wrong.

And anon king Arthur drew him with his host down by the seaside westward, toward Salisbury. And there was a day assigned betwixt king Arthur and sir Mordred, that they should meet upon a down beside Salisbury and not far from the seaside. And this day was assigned on Monday after Trinity Sunday, whereof king Arthur was passing glad that he might be avenged upon sir Mordred.

Then sir Mordred araised much people about London, for they of Kent, Sussex and Surrey, Essex, Suffolk and Norfolk held the most party with sir Mordred. And many a full noble knight drew unto him and also the king; but they that loved sir Lancelot drew unto sir Mordred.

So upon Trinity Sunday at night king Arthur dreamed a wonderful dream. And in his dream him seemed that he saw upon a chafflet a chair, and the chair was fast to a wheel, and thereupon sat king Arthur in the richest cloth of gold that might be made. And the king thought there was under him, far from him, an hideous deep black water, and therein was all manner of serpents and worms and wild beasts foul and horrible. And suddenly the king thought that the wheel turned up-so-down, and he fell among the serpents, and every beast took him by a limb. And then the king cried as he lay in his bed, 'Help! help!' and then knights, squires and yeomen awaked the king, and then he was so amazed that he wist not where he was.

And then so he awaked until it was nigh day, and then he fell on slumbering again, not sleeping nor thoroughly waking. So the king seemed verily that there came sir Gawain unto him with a number of fair ladies with him. So when king Arthur saw him he said, 'Welcome, my sister's son, I weened ye had been dead! And now I see thee on live, much am I beholden unto Almighty Jesu. Ah, fair nephew, what been these ladies that hither be come with you?'

'Sir,' said sir Gawain, 'all these be ladies for whom I have foughten for, when I was man living. And all these are tho that I did battle for in righteous quarrels, and God hath given them that grace at their great prayer, because I did battle for them for their right, that they should bring me hither unto you. Thus much hath given me leave God for to warn you of your death: for and ye fight as to-morn with sir Mordred, as ye both have assigned, doubt ye not ye shall be slain, and the most party of your people on both parties. And for the great grace and goodness that Almighty Jesu hath unto you, and for pity of you and many mo other good men there shall be slain, God hath sent me to you of his special grace to give you warning that in no wise ye do battle as to-morn, but that ye take a treatise for a month day. And proffer you largely, so that to-morn ye put in a delay. For within a month shall come sir Lancelot with all his noble knights, and rescue you worshipfully and slay sir Mordred and all that ever will hold with him.'

Then sir Gawain and all the ladies vanished, and anon the king called upon his knights, squires, and yeomen, and charged them wightly to fetch his noble lords and wise bishops unto him. And when they were come the king told them of his avision, that sir Gawain had told him and warned him that and he fought on the morn, he should be slain. Then the king commanded sir Lucan the Butler and his brother sir Bedivere the Bold, with two bishops with them, and charged them in any wise to take a treatise for a month day with sir Mordred: 'And spare not. Proffer him lands and goods as much as ye think reasonable.'

So then they departed and came to sir Mordred where he had a grim host of an hundred thousand men,* and there they entreated sir Mordred long time. And at the last sir Mordred was agreed for to have Cornwall and Kent by king Arthur's days; and after that all England, after the days of king Arthur.

Then were they condescend that king Arthur and sir Mordred should meet betwixt both their hosts, and every of them should bring fourteen persons. And so they came with this word unto Arthur. Then said he, 'I am glad that this is done.' And so he went into the field.

And when king Arthur should depart he warned all his host that and they see any sword drawn, 'look ye come on fiercely and slay that traitor, sir Mordred, for I in no wise trust him.' In like wise sir Mordred warned his host 'that and ye see any manner of sword drawn, look that ye come on fiercely and so slay all that ever before you standeth, for in no wise I will not trust for this treatise.' And in the same wise said sir Mordred unto his host: 'for I know well my father will be avenged upon me.'

And so they met as their appointment was, and were agreed and accorded thoroughly. And wine was fetched, and they drank together. Right so came out an adder of a little heath bush, and it stung a knight in the foot. And so when the knight felt him so stung, he looked down and saw the adder; and anon he drew his sword to slay the adder, and thought none other harm. And when the host on both parties saw that sword drawn, then they blew bemes, trumpets and horns, and shouted grimly, and so both hosts dressed them togethers. And king Arthur took his horse and said, 'Alas, this unhappy day!' and so rode to his party, and sir Mordred in like wise.

And never since was there never seen a more dolefuller battle in no Christian land, for there was but rushing and riding, foining and striking, and many a grim word was there spoken of either to other, and many a deadly stroke. But ever king Arthur rode throughout the battle of sir Mordred many times and did full nobly, as a noble king should do, and at all times he fainted never. And sir Mordred did his devoir that day and put himself in great peril.

And thus they fought all the long day, and never stinted till the noble knights were laid to the cold earth. And ever they fought still till it was near night, and by then was there an hundred thousand laid dead upon the earth. Then was king Arthur wood wroth out of measure, when he saw his people so slain from him. And so he looked about him and could see no mo of all his host and good knights left, no mo on live but two knights: the tone was sir Lucan de Butler and his brother sir Bedivere; and yet they were full sore wounded.

'Jesu mercy!' said the king, 'where are all my noble knights become? Alas, that ever I should see this doleful day! For now,' said king Arthur, 'I am come to mine end. But would to God,' said he, 'that I wist now where were that traitor sir Mordred that hath caused all this mischief.'

Then king Arthur looked about and was ware where stood sir Mordred leaning upon his sword among a great heap of dead men. 'Now, give me my spear,' said king Arthur unto sir Lucan, 'for yonder I have espied the traitor that all this woe hath wrought.'

'Sir, let him be,' said sir Lucan, 'for he is unhappy. And if ye pass this unhappy day ye shall be right well revenged upon him.* Good lord, remember ye of your night's dream and what the spirit of sir Gawain told you to-night, and yet God of His great goodness hath preserved you hitherto. And for God's sake, my lord, leave off this, for, blessed be God, ye have won the field. For yet we been here three on live, and with sir Mordred is not one of live. And therefore if ye leave off now, this wicked day of Destiny is past!'

'Now tide me death, tide me life,' said the king, 'now I see him yonder alone, he shall never escape mine hands! For at a better avail shall I never have him.'

'God speed you well!' said sir Bedivere.

Then the king got his spear in both his hands, and ran toward sir Mordred, crying and saying, 'Traitor, now is thy death-day come!'

And when sir Mordred saw king Arthur he ran until him with his sword drawn in his hand, and there king Arthur smote sir Mordred under the shield, with a foin of his spear, throughout the body more than a fathom. And when sir Mordred felt that he had his death's wound he thrust himself with the might that he had up to the burr of king Arthur's spear, and right so he smote his father, king Arthur, with his sword holding in both his hands, upon the side of the head, that the sword pierced the helmet and the tay of the brain. And therwith Mordred dashed down stark dead to the earth.

And noble king Arthur fell in a swough to the earth, and there he swooned oftentimes, and sir Lucan and sir Bedivere oft-times hove him up. And so weakly betwixt them they led him to a little chapel not far from the sea, and when the king was there, him thought him reasonably eased.

Then heard they people cry in the field. 'Now go thou, sir Lucan,' said the king, 'and do me to wit what betokens that noise in the field.' So sir Lucan departed, for he was grievously wounded in many places. And so as he yode he saw and hearkened by the moonlight how that pillers and robbers were come into the field to pill and to rob many a full noble knight of brooches and bees and of many a good ring and many a rich jewel. And who that were not dead all out, there they slew them for their harness and their riches.

When sir Lucan understood this work he came to the king as soon as he might, and told him all what he had heard and seen. 'Therefore by my rede,' said sir Lucan, 'it is best that we bring you to some town.'

'I would it were so,' said the king, 'but I may not stand, my head works so. Ah, sir Lancelot!' said king Arthur, 'this day have I sore missed thee! And alas, that ever I was against thee! For now have I my death, whereof sir Gawain me warned in my dream.'

Then sir Lucan took up the king the tone party and sir Bedivere the other party. And in the lifting up the king swooned, and in the lifting sir Lucan fell in a swoon, that part of his guts fell out of his body, and therewith the noble knight his heart burst. And when the king awoke he beheld sir Lucan, how he lay foaming at the mouth and part of his guts lay at his feet.

'Alas,' said the king, 'this is to me a full heavy sight, to see this noble duke so die for my sake, for he would have holpen me that had more need of help than I! Alas, that he would not complain him, for his heart was so set to help me. Now Jesu have mercy upon his soul!'

Then sir Bedivere wept for the death of his brother.

'Now leave this mourning and weeping, gentle knight,' said the king, 'for all this will not avail me. For wit thou well, and I might live myself, the death of sir Lucan would grieve me evermore. But my time hieth* fast,' said the king. 'Therefore,' said king Arthur unto sir Bedivere, 'take thou here Excaliber, my good sword, and go with it to yonder water's side. And when thou comest there, I charge thee throw my sword in that water, and come again and tell me what thou seest there.'

'My lord,' said sir Bedivere, 'your commandment shall be done, and lightly bring you word again.' So sir Bedivere departed. And by the way he beheld that noble sword, and the pommel and the haft was all precious stones. And then he said to himself, 'If I throw this rich sword in the water, thereof shall never come good, but harm and loss.' And then sir Bedivere hid Excaliber under a tree. And so as soon as he might he came again unto the king and said he had been at the water and had thrown the sword into the water.

'What saw thou there?' said the king.

'Sir,' he said, 'I saw nothing but waves and winds.'

'That is untruly said of thee,' said the king, 'and therefore go thou lightly again, and do my commandment. As thou art to me lief and dear, spare not, but throw it in.'

Then sir Bedivere returned again and took the sword in his hand; and yet him thought sin and shame to throw away that noble sword. And so eft he hid the sword and returned again and told the king that he had been at the water and done his commandment.

'What sawest thou there?' said the king.

'Sir,' he said, 'I saw nothing but waters wap and waves wan.'

'Ah, traitor unto me and untrue,' said king Arthur, 'now hast thou betrayed me twice! Who would ween that thou that hast been to me so lief and dear, and also named so noble a knight, that thou would betray me for the riches of this sword? But now go again lightly; for thy long tarrying putteth me in great jeopardy of my life, for I have taken cold. And but if thou do now as I bid thee, if ever I may see thee, I shall slay thee mine own hands, for thou wouldst for my rich sword see me dead.'

Then sir Bedivere departed and went to the sword and lightly took it up, and so he went unto the water's side. And there he bound the girdle about the hilts, and threw the sword as far into the water as he might. And there came an arm and an hand above the water, and took it and cleight it, and shook it thrice and brandished, and then vanished with the sword into the water.

So sir Bedivere came again to the king and told him what he saw. 'Alas,' said the king, 'help me hence, for I dread me I have tarried over long.'

Then sir Bedivere took the king upon his back and so went with him to the water's side. And when they were there, even fast by the bank hoved a little barge with many fair ladies in it, and among them all was a queen, and all they had black hoods. And all they wept and shrieked when they saw king Arthur.

'Now put me into that barge,' said the king. And so he did softly, and there received him three ladies with great mourning. And so they set them down, and in one of their laps king Arthur laid his head.

And then the queen said, 'Ah, my dear brother, why have ye tarried so long from me? Alas, this wound on your head hath caught overmuch cold!' And anon they rowed fromward the land, and sir Bedivere beheld all tho ladies go froward him. Then sir Bedivere cried and said,

'Ah, my lord Arthur, what shall become of me, now ye go from me and leave me here alone among mine enemies?'

'Comfort thyself,' said the king, 'and do as well as thou mayest, for in me is no trust for to trust in. For I must into the vale of Avilion to heal me of my grievous wound. And if thou hear nevermore of me, pray for my soul!'

But ever the queen and ladies wept and shrieked that it was pity to hear. And as soon as sir Bedivere had lost the sight of the barge he wept and wailed, and so took the forest and went all that night.

And in the morning he was ware, betwixt two holts hoar, of a chapel and an hermitage. Then was sir Bedivere fain, and thither he went, and when he came into the chapel he saw where lay an hermit groveling on all fours, fast thereby a tomb was new graven. When the hermit saw sir Bedivere he knew him well, for he was but little tofore Bishop of Canterbury that sir Mordred flemed.

'Sir,' said sir Bedivere, 'what man is there here interred that ye pray so fast for?'

'Fair son,' said the hermit, 'I wot not verily but by deeming. But this same night, at midnight, here came a number of ladies and brought here a dead corpse and prayed me to inter him. And here they offered an hundred tapers, and they gave me a thousand besants.'

'Alas,' said sir Bedivere, 'that was my lord king Arthur, which lieth here graven in this chapel.' Then sir Bedivere swooned. And when he awoke he prayed the hermit that he might abide with him still, there to live with fasting and prayers: 'For from hence will I never go,' said sir Bedivere, 'by my will, but all the days of my life here to pray for my lord Arthur.'

'Sir, ye are welcome to me,' said the hermit, 'for I know you better than ye ween that I do: for ye are sir Bedivere the Bold, and the full noble duke sir Lucan de Butler was your brother.' Then sir Bedivere told the hermit all as ye have heard tofore, and so he beleft with the hermit that was beforehand Bishop of Canterbury. And there sir Bedivere put upon him poor clothes, and served the hermit full lowly in fasting and in prayers.

Thus of Arthur I find no more written in books that been authorised, nother more of the very certainty of his death heard I never read. But thus was he led away in a ship wherein were three queens; that one was king Arthur sister, queen Morgan le Fay, the tother was queen of North Wales, and the third was the queen of the Waste Lands. Also there was dame Ninive, the chief lady of the lake, which had wedded sir Pelleas, the good knight; and this lady had done much for king Arthur. And this dame Ninive would never suffer sir Pelleas to be in no place where he should be in danger of his life, and so he lived unto the uttermost of his days with her in great rest.

Now more of the death of king Arthur could I never find, but that these ladies brought him to his grave, and such one was interred there which the hermit bore witness that sometime was Bishop of Canterbury. But yet the hermit knew not in certain that he was verily the body of king Arthur; for this tale sir Bedivere, a knight of the Table Round, made it to be written.

Yet some men say in many parts of England that king Arthur is not dead, but had by the will of our Lord Jesu into another place. And men say that he shall come again, and he shall win the Holy Cross. Yet I will not say that it shall be so, but rather I would say: here in this world he changed his life. And many men say that there is written upon his tomb this verse:*

HIC IACET ARTHURUS, REX QUONDAM REXQUE FUTURUS.

And thus leave I here sir Bedivere with the hermit that dwelled that time in a chapel besides Glastonbury, and there was his hermitage. And so they lived in prayers and fastings and great abstinence.

And when queen Guenevere understood that king Arthur was dead and all the noble knights, sir Mordred and all the remnant, then she stole away with five ladies with her, and so she went to Amesbury. And there she let make herself a nun, and weared white clothes and black, and great penance she took upon her, as ever did sinful woman in this land. And never creature could make her merry, but ever she lived in fasting, prayers, and alms-deeds, that all manner of people marvelled how virtuously she was changed.

5. The Dolorous Death and Departing out of this World of Sir Lancelot and Queen Guenevere

(Caxton XXI, 8–13)

Now leave we the queen in Amesbury, a nun in white clothes and black, and there she was abbess and ruler, as reason would. And now turn we from her and speak we of sir Lancelot du Lake, that when he heard in his country that sir Mordred was crowned king in England and made war against king Arthur, his own father, and would let him to land in his own land (also it was told him how sir Mordred had laid a siege about the Tower of London, because the queen would not wed him), then was sir Lancelot wroth out of measure and said to his kinsmen,

'Alas! that double traitor, sir Mordred! Now me repenteth that ever he escaped my hands, for much shame hath he done unto my lord Arthur. For I feel by this doleful letter that sir Gawain sent me, on whose soul Jesu have mercy, that my lord Arthur is full hard bestead. Alas,' said sir Lancelot, 'that ever I should live to hear of that most noble king that made me knight thus to be overset with his subject in his own realm! And this doleful letter that my lord sir Gawain hath sent me afore his death, praying me to see his tomb, wit you well his doleful words shall never go from my heart. For he was a full noble knight as ever was born! And in an unhappy hour was I born that ever I should have that mishap to slay first sir Gawain, sir Gaheris, the good knight, and mine own friend sir Gareth that was a full noble knight.

Now, alas, I may say I am unhappy that ever I should do thus. And yet, alas, might I never have hap to slay that traitor, sir Mordred!'

'Now leave your complaints,' said sir Bors, 'and first revenge you of the death of sir Gawain, on whose soul Jesu have mercy! And it will be well done that ye see his tomb, and secondly that ye revenge my lord Arthur and my lady queen Guenevere.'

'I thank you,' said sir Lancelot, 'for ever ye will my worship.'

Then they made them ready in all haste that might be, with ships and galleys, with him and his host to pass into England. And so he passed over the sea till* he came to Dover, and there he landed with seven kings, and the number was hideous to behold.

Then sir Lancelot spiered of men of Dover where was the king become. And anon the people told him how he was slain, and sir Mordred too, with an hundred thousand that died upon a day; and how sir Mordred gave king Arthur the first battle there at his landing, and there was sir Gawain slain: 'And upon the morn sir Mordred fought with the king on Barham Down, and there the king put sir Mordred to the wars.'

'Alas,' said sir Lancelot, 'this is the heaviest tidings that ever came to my heart! Now, fair sirs,' said sir Lancelot, 'show me the tomb of sir Gawain.' And anon he was brought into the castle of Dover, and so they showed him the tomb. Then sir Lancelot kneeled down by the tomb and wept, and prayed heartily for his soul.

And that night he let make a dole, and all that would come of the town or of the country they had as much flesh and fish and wine and ale, and every man and woman he dealt to twelve pence, come whoso would. Thus with his own hand dealt he this money, in a mourning gown. And ever he wept heartily and prayed the people to pray for the soul of sir Gawain.

And on the morn all the priests and clerks that might be gotten in the country and in the town were there, and sang masses of requiem. And there offered first sir Lancelot, and he offered an hundred pound, and then the seven kings offered, and every of them offered forty pound. Also there was a thousand knights, and every of them offered a pound; and the offering dured from the morn to night.

And there sir Lancelot lay two nights upon his tomb in prayers and in doleful weeping. Then on the third day, sir Lancelot called the kings dukes and earls, with the barons and all his noble knights, and said thus:

'My fair lords, I thank you all of your coming into this country with me. But wit you well all, we are come too late, and that shall repent me while I live; but against death may no man rebel. But sithen it is so,' said sir Lancelot, 'I will myself ride and seek my lady, queen Guenevere. For, as I hear say, she hath had great pain and much disease, and I hear say that she is fled into the west. And therefore ye shall all abide me here, and but if I come again within these fifteen days, take your ships and your fellowship and depart into your country, for I will do as I say you.'

Then came sir Bors and said, 'My lord, sir Lancelot, what think ye for to do, now for to ride in this realm? Wit you well ye shall* find few friends.'

'Be as be may, as for that,' said sir Lancelot. 'Keep you still here, for I will forth on my journey, and no man nor child shall go with me.' So it was no boot to strive, but he departed and rode westerly; and there he sought a seven or eight days.

And at the last he came to a nunnery, and anon queen Guenevere was ware of sir Lancelot as she walked in the cloister. And anon as she saw him there, she swooned thrice, that all ladies and gentlewomen had work enough to hold the queen from the earth. So when she might speak she called her ladies and gentlewomen to her, and then she said thus:

'Ye marvel, fair ladies, why I make this fare. Truly,' she said, 'it is for the sight of yonder knight that yonder standeth. Wherefore I pray you call him hither to me.'

Then sir Lancelot was brought before her. Then the queen said to all tho ladies:

'Through this same man and me hath all this war be wrought, and the death of the most noblest knights of the world; for through our love that we have loved together is my most noble lord slain. Therefore, sir Lancelot, wit thou well I am set in such a plight to get my soul heal. And yet I trust, through God's grace and through His Passion of His wounds wide, that after my death I may have a sight of the blessed face of Christ Jesu, and on Doomsday to sit on His right side; for as sinful as ever I was, now are saints in heaven. And therefore, sir Lancelot, I require thee and beseech thee heartily, for all the love that ever was betwixt us, that thou never see me no more in the visage. And I command thee, on God's behalf, that thou forsake my company.

And to thy kingdom look thou turn again, and keep well thy realm from war and wrack, for as well as I have loved thee heretofore mine heart will not serve now to see thee; for through thee and me is the flower of kings and knights destroyed. And therefore go thou to thy realm, and there take thee* a wife, and live with her with joy and bliss. And I pray thee heartily to pray for me to the Everlasting Lord that I may amend my mis-living.'

'Now, my sweet madam,' said sir Lancelot, 'would ye that I should turn again unto my country, and there to wed a lady? Nay, madam, wit you well, that shall I never do, for I shall never be so false unto you of that I have promised. But the self destiny that ye have taken you to, I will take me to, for to please Jesu,* and ever for you I cast me specially to pray.'

'Ah, sir Lancelot, if ye will do so, hold thy promise! But I may never believe you,' said the queen, 'but that ye will turn to the world again.'*

'Well, madam,' said he, 'ye say as it pleaseth you, for yet wist ye me never false of my promise. And God defend but that I should forsake the world as ye have done! For in the quest of the Sankgreall I had that time forsaken the vanities of the world, had not your love been. And if I had done so at that time with my heart, will, and thought, I had passed all the knights that ever were in the Sankgreall except sir Galahad, my son. And therefore, lady, sithen ye have taken you to perfection, I must needs take me to perfection, of right. For I take record of God, in you I have had mine earthly joy, and if I had founden you now so disposed, I had cast me to have had you into mine own royame. But sithen I find you thus disposed, I ensure you faithfully, I will ever take me to penance, and pray while my life lasteth, if that I may find any hermit, other grey or white, that will receive me. Wherefore, madam, I pray you kiss me, and never no more.'

'Nay,' said the queen, 'that shall I never do, but abstain you from such works.'

And they departed; but there was never so hard an hearted man but he would have wept to see the dolour that they made, for there was lamentation as they had be stungen with spears, and many times they swooned. And the ladies bore the queen to her chamber.

And sir Lancelot awoke, and went and took his horse, and rode all that day and all night in a forest, weeping. And at last he was ware of an hermitage and a chapel stood betwixt two cliffs, and then he heard a little bell ring to mass. And thither he rode and alight, and tied his horse to the gate and heard mass.

And he that sang was the Bishop of Canterbury. Both the Bishop and sir Bedivere knew sir Lancelot, and they spoke togethers after mass. But when sir Bedivere had told his tale all whole, sir Lancelot's heart almost burst for sorrow, and sir Lancelot threw his arms abroad, and said, 'Alas! Who may trust this world?'

And then he kneeled down on his knee and prayed the Bishop to shrive him and assoil him. And then he besought the Bishop that he might be his brother. Then the Bishop said, 'I will gladly,' and there he put an habit upon sir Lancelot. And there he served God day and night with prayers and fastings.

Thus the great host abode at Dover. And then sir Lionel took fifteen lords with him and rode to London to seek sir Lancelot; and there sir Lionel was slain and many of his lords. Then sir Bors de Ganis made the great host for to go home again, and sir Bors, sir Ector de Maris, sir Blamour, sir Bleoberis, with mo other of sir Lancelot's kin, took on them to ride all England overthwart and endlong to seek sir Lancelot.

So sir Bors by fortune rode so long till he came to the same chapel where sir Lancelot was. And so sir Bors heard a little bell knell that rang to mass, and there he alight and heard mass. And when mass was done, the Bishop, sir Lancelot and sir Bedivere came to sir Bors, and when sir Bors saw sir Lancelot in that manner clothing, then he prayed the Bishop that he might be in the same suit. And so there was an habit put upon him, and there he lived in prayers and fasting.

And within half a year there was come sir Galihud, sir Galihodin, sir Blamour, sir Bleoberis, sir Villiers, sir Clarrus, and sir Gahalantine. So all these seven noble knights there abode still. And when they saw sir Lancelot had taken him to such perfection they had no lust to depart but took such an habit as he had.

Thus they endured in great penance six year. And then sir Lancelot took the habit of priesthood of the Bishop, and a twelve-month he sang mass. And there was none of these other knights but they read in books and holp for to sing mass, and rang bells, and did lowly all manner of service. And so their horses went where they would, for they took no regard of no worldly richesses. For when they saw sir Lancelot endure such penance in prayers and fastings they took no force what pain they endured, for to see the noblest knight of the world take such abstinence that he waxed full lean.

And thus upon a night there came a vision to sir Lancelot and charged him, in remission of his sins, to haste him unto Amesbury: 'And by then thou come there, thou shalt find queen Guenevere dead. And therefore take thy fellows with thee, and purvey them of an horse-bier, and fetch thou the corpse of her, and bury her by her husband, the noble king Arthur.' So this avision came to Lancelot thrice in one night. Then sir Lancelot rose up or day and told the hermit. 'It were well done,' said the hermit, 'that ye made you ready and that ye disobey not the avision.' Then sir Lancelot took his seven fellows with him, and on foot they yede from Glastonbury to Amesbury, the which is little more than thirty mile, and thither they came within two days, for they were weak and feeble to go.

And when sir Lancelot was come to Amesbury within the nunnery queen Guenevere died but half an hour afore. And the ladies told sir Lancelot that queen Guenevere told them all or she passed that sir Lancelot had been priest near a twelve-month: 'and hither he cometh as fast as he may to fetch my corpse, and beside my lord king Arthur he shall bury me.' Wherefore the queen said in hearing of them all, 'I beseech Almighty God that I may never have power to see sir Lancelot with my worldly eyen!' 'And thus,' said all the ladies, 'was ever her prayer these two days till she was dead.'

Then sir Lancelot saw her visage, but he wept not greatly, but sighed. And so he did all the observance of the service himself, both the dirge and on the morn he sang mass. And there was ordained an horse-bier, and so with an hundred torches ever burning about the corpse of the queen and ever sir Lancelot with his eight fellows went about the horse-bier, singing and reading many an holy orison, and frankincense upon the corpse incensed.

Thus sir Lancelot and his eight fellows went on foot from Amesbury unto Glastonbury; and when they were come to the chapel and the hermitage, there she had a dirge with great devotion. And on the morn the hermit that sometime was Bishop of Canterbury sang the mass of requiem with great devotion, and sir Lancelot was the first that offered, and then also his eight fellows. And then she was wrapped in cered cloth of Rennes from the top to the toe, in thirtyfold; and after she was put in a web of lead, and then in a coffin of marble.

And when she was put in the earth sir Lancelot swooned, and lay long still, while the hermit came and awaked him, and said, 'Ye be to blame, for ye displease God with such manner of sorrow-making.'

'Truly,' said sir Lancelot, 'I trust I do not displease God, for He knoweth mine intent. For my sorrow was not, nor is not, for any rejoicing of sin, but my sorrow may never have end. For when I remember of her beauty and of her noblesse, that was both with her king and with her, so when I saw his corpse and her corpse so lie togethers, truly mine heart would not serve to sustain my care-full body. Also when I remember me how by my default and mine orgule and my pride that they were both laid full low, that were peerless that ever was living of Christian people, wit you well,' said sir Lancelot, 'this remembered, of their kindness and mine unkindness, sank so to mine heart that I might not sustain myself.' So the French book maketh mention.

Then sir Lancelot never after ate but little meat, nor drank, till he was dead, for then he sickened more and more and dried and dwined away. For the Bishop nor none of his fellows might not make him to eat and little he drank, that he was waxen by a cubit shorter than he was, that the people could not know him. For evermore, day and night, he prayed, but sometime he slumbered a broken sleep. Ever he was lying grovelling on the tomb of king Arthur and queen Guenevere, and there was no comfort that the Bishop, nor sir Bors, nor none of his fellows could make him, it availed not.

So within six weeks after, sir Lancelot fell sick and lay in his bed. And then he sent for the Bishop that there was hermit, and all his true fellows. Then sir Lancelot said with dreary steven, 'Sir Bishop, I pray you give to me all my rights that longeth to a Christian man.'

'It shall not need you,' said the hermit and all his fellows. 'It is but heaviness of your blood. Ye shall be well mended by the grace of God to-morn.'

'My fair lords,' said sir Lancelot, 'wit you well my care-full body will into the earth. I have warning more than now I will say. Therefore give me my rights.'

So when he was houseled and aneled and had all that a Christian man ought to have, he prayed the Bishop that his fellows might bear his body to Joyous Gard. (Some men say it was Alnwick and some men say it was Bamborough.) 'Howbeit,' said sir Lancelot, 'me repenteth

sore, but I made mine avow sometime that in Joyous Gard I would
be buried. And because of breaking of mine avow, I pray you all,
lead me thither.' Then there was weeping and wringing of hands among
his fellows.

So at a season of the night they all went to their beds, for they all
lay in one chamber. And so after midnight, against day, the Bishop
that was hermit, as he lay in his bed asleep, he fell upon a great laughter.
And therewith all the fellowship awoke and came to the Bishop and
asked him what he ailed.

'Ah, Jesu mercy!' said the Bishop, 'why did ye awake me? I was
never in all my life so merry and so well at ease.' 'Wherefore?' said
sir Bors.

'Truly,' said the Bishop, 'here was sir Lancelot with me, with mo
angels than ever I saw men in one day. And I saw the angels heave
up sir Lancelot unto heaven, and the gates of heaven opened against
him.' 'It is but dretching of swevens,' said sir Bors, 'for I doubt not
sir Lancelot aileth nothing but good.' 'It may well be,' said the Bishop.
'Go ye to his bed, and then shall ye prove the sooth.'

So when sir Bors and his fellows came to his bed they found him
stark dead; and he lay as he had smiled, and the sweetest savour about
him that ever they felt. Then was there weeping and wringing of hands,
and the greatest dole they made that ever made men.

And on the morn the Bishop did his mass of requiem, and after the
Bishop and all the nine knights put sir Lancelot in the same horse-bier
that queen Guenevere was laid in tofore that she was buried. And so
the Bishop and they all togethers went with the body of sir Lancelot
daily, till they came to Joyous Gard; and ever they had an hundred
torches burning about him.

And so within fifteen days they came to Joyous Gard. And there
they laid his corpse in the body of the choir, and sang and read many
psalters and prayers over him and about him. And ever his visage was
laid open and naked, that all folks might behold him, for such was the
custom in tho days, that all men of worship should so lie with open
visage till that they were buried.

And right thus as they were at their service, there came sir Ector de
Maris that had seven year sought all England, Scotland, and Wales,
seeking his brother, sir Lancelot. And when sir Ector heard such noise
and light in the choir of Joyous Gard, he alight and put his horse from

him and came into the choir. And there he saw men sing and weep. And all they knew sir Ector, but he knew not them. Then went sir Bors unto sir Ector and told him how there lay his brother, sir Lancelot, dead. And then sir Ector threw his shield, sword, and helm from him, and when he beheld sir Lancelot's visage he fell down in a swoon. And when he waked it were hard any tongue to tell the doleful complaints that he made for his brother.

'Ah, Lancelot!' he said, 'thou were head of all Christian knights! And now I dare say,' said sir Ector, 'thou sir Lancelot, there thou liest, that thou were never matched of earthly knight's hand. And thou were the courteoust knight that ever bore shield! And thou were the truest friend to thy lover that ever bestrode horse, and thou were the truest lover of a sinful man that ever loved woman, and thou were the kindest man that ever struck with sword. And thou were the goodliest person that ever came among press of knights, and thou was the meekest man and the gentlest that ever ate in hall among ladies, and thou were the sternest knight to thy mortal foe that ever put spear in the rest.'

Then there was weeping and dolour out of measure.

Thus they kept sir Lancelot's corpse on-loft fifteen days, and then they buried it with great devotion. And then at leisure they went all with the Bishop of Canterbury to his hermitage, and there they were together more than a month.

Then sir Constantine that was sir Cador's son of Cornwall was chosen king of England, and he was a full noble knight, and worshipfully he ruled this royame. And then this king Constantine sent for the Bishop of Canterbury, for he heard say where he was. And so he was restored unto his bishopric and left that hermitage, and sir Bedivere was there ever still hermit to his life's end.

Then sir Bors de Ganis, sir Ector de Maris, sir Gahalantine, sir Galihud, sir Galihodin, sir Blamour, sir Bleoberis, sir Villiers le Valiant, sir Clarrus of Cleremont, all these knights drew them to their countries. Howbeit king Constantine would have had them with him, but they would not abide in this royame. And there they all lived in their countries as holy men.

And some English books maken mention that they went never out of England after the death of sir Lancelot—but that was but favour of makers. For the French book maketh mention, and is authorised, that sir Bors, sir Ector, sir Blamour and sir Bleoberis went into the Holy Land, thereas Jesu Christ was quick and dead. And anon as they had established their lands (for, the book saith, so sir Lancelot commanded them for to do or ever he passed out of this world), there these four knights did many battle upon the miscreants, or Turks. And there they died upon a Good Friday, for God's sake.

Here is the end of the whole book of king Arthur and of his noble knights of the Round Table, that when they were wholly togethers there was ever an hundred and forty. And here is the end of the *Death of Arthur*

I pray you all gentlemen and gentlewomen that readeth this book of Arthur and his knights from the beginning to the ending, pray for me while I am on live that God send me good deliverance. And when I am dead, I pray you all pray for my soul.

For this book was ended the ninth year of the reign of king Edward the Fourth, by sir Thomas Malory, knight, as Jesu help him for his great might, as he is the servant of Jesu both day and night.

CAXTON'S COLOPHON

Thus endeth this noble and joyous book entitled *Le Morte Darthur*; notwithstanding it treateth of the birth, life and acts of the said king Arthur, of his noble knights of the Round Table, their marvellous enquests and adventures, th'achieving of the Sangreal, and in th'end the dolorous death and departing out of this world of them all. Which book was reduced into English by sir Thomas Malory, knight, as afore is said, and by me divided into XXI books, chaptered and enprinted and finished in th' Abbey Westminster, the last day of July, the year of our Lord MCCCCLXXXV.

Caxton me fieri fecit.

NOTES ON CAXTON'S PREFACE

Page 44. *Polychronicon*. A universal history written in Latin by Ranulf Higden, monk of Chester (c. 1299– c. 1363), very popular in the fifteenth century, of which a translation with additions was printed by Caxton in 1482.

Bochas. Giovanni Boccaccio, 1313–1375, author of the *Decamerone*, was principally famous in his own and the following two centuries for learned Latin works, of which *De Casu Principum* or *De Casibus Virorum Illustrium* (*Of the Falls of Princes*) was one of the best known.

Galfridus in his British book. Geoffrey of Monmouth, *Historia Regum Britanniae*. See Introduction.

Page 45. '*all is written for our doctrine*'. A remark frequently reiterated by medieval writers. Cf. Chaucer, *Nun's Priest's Tale* (ed. F. Robinson, 1957), VII, 3441–2. It comes from St. Paul, *Romans* 15:4.

NOTES ON '*THE MORTE DARTHUR*'

(*V* indicates Professor Vinaver's comment in the *Works*. *M* indicates Malory or his text. *C* indicates Caxton or his text. *W* indicates the Winchester MS.)

The asterisk is used to mark all variation from Vinaver's edition of *W*. See Introduction, p. 37.

Page 48. *Camelot*. The identification of Camelot with Winchester is *M*'s own. (*V*)

Page 72. *had abated, etc.* Set her dog to attack a barren hind so that it could be shot with bow and arrow (*V*).

checked it, etc. V suggests = 'came to a check because the cry of a hound told them that the hind had been brought to bay at a stream'. *M*'s phrase is elliptical, perhaps because it is technical hunting language, unnoticed by the dictionaries. Or perhaps we have here an example of *M*'s masterful and occasionally idiosyncratic way with syntax.

came to the well, etc. The hind went to ground in the stream from the spring, to cool herself and kill the scent (*V*).

Page 74. *nine knights. V* points out that ten are named in *W*, eight in *C*. Here as elsewhere (cf. e.g. pp. 107, 153 ff.) numbers do not correspond with names named, and even change in the course of the story. It would seem that this kind of realism did not much interest medieval writers and readers; also Roman numerals were easily mistaken.

Page 78. *And thus it passed, etc.* The Maying, and *M*'s reflections, seem to be *M*'s own.

Page 83. *chariot* for the more usual *cart* is presumably due to the influence of the French.

Page 94.   *the French book. V* points out that the episode of Sir Urry is virtually *M*'s own invention, like *The Great Tournament*. Each of these episodes is necessary to *M*'s own structure. Mention of 'the French book' often suggests that *M* is inventing.

Page 96.   *Then many kings, etc.; Then came many others*; each of these editorial phrases summarizes *M*'s long lists of knights, which are only meaningless names in the context of the present selection. But they refer to many past adventures in 'the whole book', and in the economy of the whole provide a roll-call and summary of the great men and achievements of the Round Table, brought together to emphasize the greatness of the Round Table, and therefore the supreme achievement of Lancelot. Cf. Introduction.

very many other good knights. Another list is summarized by the editor here. Malory is fond of lists of names, which he introduces independent of his sources. It is a device many great writers have valued.

Page 99.   *because I have lost, etc. M* perhaps felt he needed to apologize for omitting material which was clearly not to his purpose, but which the reader might expect. Direct authorial comment to the reader or listener, which in a modern printed book would be placed in a preface or even on the book wrapper *outside* the story, in order to preserve the illusion *within* the story, is often, in medieval fiction, included within the story. Medieval works of fiction thus include more levels of reality than modern works. Chaucer's poetry, e.g. *Troilus and Criseyde*, is the obvious example, where the poem begins and ends with a direct address to the audience on a different level of reality from the fictional story. The poem is longer than the story. So here, in a similar though not identical way, Malory comments, at a convenient pause, on the process of his story, while it is still continuing. There is no difficulty so long as we realise he is not writing a modern novel.

on the other side. In the original manuscript the new section must have begun thus, but *V* points out that *W* in fact continues on the same page.

Page 139.   *Lo, ye all Englishmen, etc.* An example of direct authorial address, of *M*'s own views, and of his passionate involvement with the story. Among much in this section that is remote from the sources *V* points out that this address is entirely original.

Page 142.   *Then sir Mordred araised, etc. V* suggests that the counties who followed Mordred were the same as those which supported the Yorkists to whom *M* himself was opposed.

Page 152.   *Sankgreall. W* ends here.

Page 155.   *Alnwick . . . Bamborough.* This identification is not in *M*'s sources, but *M* himself was probably at the siege of the castles of both places, which are in Northumberland, Dec.-Jan. 1462-3. The journey of Warwick's army, with which *M* served, from London o Northumberland, took about the same time as the journey from Lancelot's hermitage to Joyous Gard, fifteen days (*V*).

me repenteth sore. He repents having made a vow to be buried in Joyous Gard.
Page 156. *because of breaking.* Here *because* = 'in order to prevent'—colloquial and perhaps idiosyncratic usage. *V* is mistaken in his note here.
Page 157. *Ah, Lancelot,* etc. *V* points, as probable model for this passage, to the comments on the death of Gawain in the alliterative *Morte Arthure*, 3872 ff., which I modernize. (Cf. Introduction)

A king asks who was Gawain, for

> He was the sternest in stour that ever steel weared.   [battle]

Mordred replies:

> He was matchless on mould, man, by my truth;   [earth]
> This was sir Gawain the good, the gladdest of other,
> And the graciousest gome that under God lived,   [man]
> Man hardiest of hand, happiest in arms,
> And the hendest in hall under heavené rich,   [most courteous: kingdom
>   of heaven]
> The lordliest of leading whiles he live might,   [conduct]
> For he was lion alosed in lands enough.   [renowned as]
> Had thou known him, sir king, in kith there he longed,   [nation]
> His cunning, his knighthood, his kindly works,   [knowledge]
> His doing, his doughtiness, his deeds of arms,
> Thou would have dole for his death the days of thy life.   [grief]

Select Glossary

Only unusual words, or the unusual meanings of modern words (which may also be found in the text but not in the Glossary in their modern, or in near-modern meanings) are recorded. In all cases the reader should consider the context.

a *v.* have (*as auxiliary*)
abated at *pp.* set on
about *adv.* in every direction; **be about to** to be scheming, to be engaged in
abroad *adv.* widely apart
accordment *n.* reconciliation
adretched *pp.* perturbed
advantage *n.* **of a great advantage** in a very superior way
adventure *n.* chance, doubt
advised *v.* **advised togethers** took counsel; *refl.* think
affiance *n.* trust
affray *n.* disturbance
aforn *adv.* previously
allegiance *n.* relief
allow *v.* commend
althers *adj. gen. pl.* of all; **your althers** of you all
and *cj.* if
aneled *pp.* given the last anointing before death, extreme unction
anon *adv.* immediately; **anon as** as soon as
appeal *v.* accuse
aretted *pp.* reckoned
array *n.* dress, state of affairs
arrest *n.* capture
arson *n.* saddle-bow
assay *v.* try, test
assoil *v.* absolve from sin
avail *n.* advantage
avaunt *n.* boast
avise *v.* see, perceive; **avised him better** looked at him more closely

avision *n.* dream-vision
avoid *v.* **avoided his horse** dismounted
await *n.* watch
await *v.* **await upon** to look out for
awaiting *pres. p.* looking out

bain *n.* bath
bait *n.* attack
barget *n.* small boat
battle *n.* army
bees *n. pl.* bracelets
behest *n.* promise
beleft *v. pret.* remained
bemes *n. pl.* trumpets
beseen *ppl. adj.* **well beseen** good looking
bestead *pp.* situated; **hard bestead** hard pressed
betime *adv.* early
betook *v. pret.* assigned
bezants *n. pl.* trumpets
big *adj.* powerful
blood *n.* kindred
blow *v.* **blow upon** slander
bobance *n.* arrogance
boot *n.* use
boteneth *v. 3 sg. impers.* does good
brim *adj.* fierce
brunts *n. pl.* heavy blows
bulls *n. pl.* **bulls under lead** papal edicts properly sealed
burgeon *v.* bud
burgess *n.* citizen
burr *n.* broad ring on spear to protect the hand

bushment *n.* ambush
but *cj.* except; but if unless

caitiff *n. as adj.* miserable
call *v.* accuse
cankered *ppl. adj.* malignant
can *v.* **can you thank** express thanks to you
case *n.* plight
cast *v. refl.* intend
cered *ppl. adj.* waxed
certain *n.* **a certain** someone
chafe *v.* irritate
chafflet *n.* platform
charge *n.* task
charged *pp.* laden
checked *v. pret.* stopped
cheer *n.* **make cheer** behave
child *n.* youth in noble service; **child of the chamber** page
cleight *v. pret.* grasped
coasted *v. pret.* followed
compare *v.* contend
compassed *v. pret.* reflected
complaints *n. pl.* expressions of sorrow
condescended *ppl. adj.* agreed
conditions *n. pl.* qualities
counsel *n,* **in counsel** in private; **of your counsel** in your confidence
courage *n.* encouragement
coursers *n. pl.* chargers
cousin germain *n.* first cousin
cross *n.* grave cross
croup *n.* hindquarters

danger *n.* power
dangerous *adj.* formidable
dare *v.* remain still
dashed *v. pret.* fell violently
deal *n.* part
deal *v.* do what is necessary
deeming *n.* suspicion, guessing
defamed *pp.* spoken publicly about
deliverly *adv.* quickly

depart *v.* part, go
depraved *pp.* disparaged
depreve *v.* convict
devise *v.* contrive
devoided *v. pret.* removed, dismounted from
devoir *n.* utmost effort
discomfit *pp.* beaten
disease *n.* trouble
disparbeled *pp.* scattered
displayed *pp.* drawn apart
distress *v.* attack
disworship *n.* dishonour
doubt *v.* fear
dole *n.* sorrow
draughts *n. pl.* recesses
dress *v. refl.* make ready; **dressed them togethers** advanced towards each other
dretching *n.* troubling
driving *pres. p.* rushing
dured *v. pret.* lasted
dwine *v.* dwindle

eaves *n. pl.* edge
eft *adv.* again
enbraid *v.* reproach
enchafe *v.* warm
endite *v.* write
endlong *adv.* from end to end
espies *n. pl.* **to make espies** to place spies
estres *n. pl.* rooms
except *v.* make exception of
eyen *n. pl.* eyes

fain *adv.* gladly
fare *n.* fuss
fear *v.* frighten
feel *v.* understand; **felt** *pret.* smelt
fellow *n.* companion
fewte *n.* track
fewtred *v. pret.* placed (spear) in rest
flemed *v. pret. and pp.* made to flee, banished
foin *v. and n.* thrust

foining *pres. p.* thrusting
forbled *pp. adj.* weak from loss of blood
forecast *n.* plot
force *n.* **no force** it does not matter; **took no force** did not care
forethink *v. refl.* regret
frick *adj.* vigorous
fro(m)ward *prep.* away from

gar *v.* command
gentle *adj.* noble
ghostly *adj.* spiritual
gibbet *n.* gallows
glaive *n.* spear
go *v.* walk
grauntmercy *int.* (*Fr.*) many thanks; **God graunt mercy** thanks be to God
grounden *ppl. adj.* sharpened
guise *n.* manner

hackneys *n. pl.* hacks, ambling horses
happed *v. pret.* happened
harness *n.* armour
height *n.* **spake on height** called at the top of his voice
hie *v.* hasten
hight *v. pret.* was called
hind *n.* female red deer
historial *adj.* historical
hold *v.* possess, press, fight
holp(en) *v. pret. and pp.* helped
holts *n. pl.* woods
honesty *n.* honour
houseled *pp.* shriven, confessed
hoved *v. pret.* waited
hurling *n.* commotion

in *prep.* in, by, near, on, because of, for, concerning, to
inlike *adv.* alike
instance *n.* entreaty
interdicting *n.* excommunication
inwith *prep.* within ·

keep *n.* **take keep** look after

keep *v.* guard
kindly *adj.* natural
kindness *n.* good nature

lain *v.* hide
large *adj.* generous
largelier *adv.* more unrestrainedly
largely *adv.* openly
laud *n.* praise
leech *n.* doctor
lep *v. pret.* leaped
let *v.* prevent; **let**+*act. inf.* order, cause+*passive inf.*
licorous *adj.* lecherous
lief *adj.* loved
liefer *adv. comp.* rather
lieve *v.* believe
light *adj.* active
light *v.* become lighter
lightly *adv.* quickly
like *v.* please; **me liketh** it pleases me
likely *adj.* handsome
list *v.* wish
long *adj.* due; **long upon** due to
longed *v. pret.* belonged
loving *n.* praise
lust *n.* desire

malgré *n.* ill-will
mal engine *n.* (*Fr.*) evil intention
maugre *prep.* in spite of; **maugre their heads** against their will
meat *n.* food
medley *n.* fight
menour *n.* behaviour
meseemeth *v. 3 sg. impers.* it seems to me
mercy *n.* (*Fr.*) thanks
meyny *n.* followers
mo *adj. comp.* more in number
more *adj. comp.* greater
most *adj. superl.* greatest

namely *adv.* especially
ne *adv. cj.* not, nor
near *adv. comp.* nearer

new-fangle *adj.* fond of novelty
nis *v. pres.* is not
notoirly *adv.* **notoirly known** extremely well-known
nother *pron. cj.* neither, nor
nought *n.* nothing

of *prep.* at, about, by, from, during, for, to, on, with, of, than
on *prep.* on, concerning, against, for, in
ones *n.* **at ones** as one
on-loft *adv.* above ground
on-side *adv.* out of the way
or *prep.* before
orgule *n.* pride
orgulous *adj.* proud
orgulust *adj. superl.* proudest
orison *n.* prayer
other *conj.* or
other *conj. pron.* either
ouches *n. pl.* ornaments
overled *pp.* oppressed
overthwart *adv.* across, from side to side
owe *v.* owe, own, ought

paid *pp.* pleased
palfrey *n.* saddle horse
pallets *n. pl.* mattresses
pardé *int.* by Heaven
parters *n. pl.* umpires
party *n.* part, side
paynim *n.* heathen
peaced *pp.* pacified
peradventure *adv.* perhaps
perform *v.* do, complete
pick *v. refl.* go away
pight *v. pret.* pitched, thrust
pill *v.* plunder
pillers *n. pl.* plunderers
plucking *vbl. n.* **plucking up** urging (horse)
pommel *n.* knob at the end of sword handle
press *n.* crowd

quarter *n.* side
quick *adj.* alive
raced *v. pret.* pulled
raised *v. pret.* rose
rasure *n.* cutting
ravish *v.* **let ravish** sent for
rearmaine *n.* back-hand stroke
record *n.* **to record** as witness; **take record of God** call God to witness
recrayed *adj.* cowardly
recreant *adj.* **to be recreant** to surrender
rede *n.* advice
rede *v.* advise
rehearse *v.* repeat
relieved *v. pret.* rallied
religious *n. pl.* monks (or nuns)
renommé *n.* renown
report *v. refl.* appeal for confirmation
reverse *adv.* with back-handed blows
roamed *v. pret.* went
royame *n.* kingdom
rumour *n.* outcry

sad *adj.* heavy
sadly *adv.* firmly
salued *v. pret.* greeted
salve *n.* medicinal ointment
salved *v. pret.* anointed
sands *n. pl.* messengers
sarps *n. pl.* chains?
saw *n.* saying, proverb
schedule *n.* letter
search *v.* probe
see *v.* look for
seemed *v. pret.* appeared
service *n.* devotion
shend *v.* harm
shortcoming *n.* rudeness
shower *n.* misfortune
shred *v.* hack
shriven *pp.* confessed
sin *adv.* since
sit *v.* endure

sith(en) *adv.* since
sleight *n.* skill
soil *n.* ground; **at the soil** gone to ground
speed *v.* help
spiered *v. pret.* asked
spiteously *adv.* grievously
spy *n.* watch
stably *adv.* firmly
stalk *n.* act of stalking game
stalled *pp.* established
steven *n.* voice
stiff *adj.* sturdy
stint *v. pret.* stopped
stirred *v. pret.* rowed
stour *n.* battle
strained *v. refl. pret.* controlled, forced
strait *adj.* narrow; *adv.* severely
straitly *adv.* severely
string *n.* leash
suffer *v.* allow
suit *n.* type of clothing
swevens *n. pl.* dreams
swough *n.* faint

tay *n.* outer part
term *n.* period
thinks *3 sg. pres. impers.* **us thinks** it seems to us
tho *adj. and pron.* those
thrang *v. pret.* pressed
tide *n.* time
till *prep.* to
tone *adj. and pron.* (the) one
tother *adj. and pron.* (the) other
traced *v. pret.* **traced and traversed** moved to and fro
trapped *ppl. adj.* adorned with trappings
treatise *n.* treaty, truce
trenchant *adj.* sharp
truncheon *n.* shaft of spear
trussed *v. pret.* equipped
tryst *n.* hunting station (for shooting game)?

umbecast *v. pret.* cast around
undern *n.* about nine a.m.; noon
undertake *v.* **I undertake** I am sure
unhap *n.* misfortune
unhappiness *n.* ill-luck
unhappy *adj.* unlucky, troublesome, disastrous
until *prep.* to
use *v.* practise
utterance *n.* utmost, end

very *adj.* true

wait *v.* **wait upon** watch out for
wan *adj.* dark
wan *v.* darken
wap *v.* lap
warn *v.* forbid, command
waxen *pp.* become
web *n.* sheet
well *n.* spring
went *v. pret.* supposed
while *cj.* until
wight *adj.* powerful
wightly *adv.* quickly
wilful *adj.* voluntary
will *v.* wish for
wise *n.* manner
wit *v.* know; **wit you well** be sure; **wist** *pret.*
wite *v.* blame
without *prep.* outside
wonderfully *adv.* with admiration
wood *adj.* mad; *adv.* furiously
woodly *adv.* madly
work *n.* matter
works *v. 3 sg.* aches
worship *n.* honour
worshipped *pp.* honoured
wot *pres. ind. of wit,* *v.* know
would *v. pret.* wanted
wrack *n.* destruction

yede, yode *v. pret.* went
yolden *pp.* yielded
ysought *pp.* sought